MW00885091

8 Weeks to Your Promotion in Your Home Party Business

How to Rapidly Qualify and Get Paid at Title
Every Single Month

Susie Nelson

Here's what others have to say about Susie Nelson's training and coaching:

My business has become so much more productive and "alive". Before these trainings, I was doing things with my business and my team to the best of my ability. Once the training started, I realized that I was not utilizing my time, talent and efforts in the most effective ways possible to continue the momentum I needed to move into the highest leadership levels with my company. I now find that my stress level is much lower due to the tools I have been provided to make my business work for me instead of me working for my business.

Dondrea Bryant - Sr. Director, ThirtyOne Gifts

I started my direct sales business about four months before I found Susie's training courses online. To try to obtain growth for my business, I had signed up to do a number of vendor events and, having no sales experience whatsoever, searched online for some guidance. I ordered Susie's 'Kick Butt Booths' training course and was so pleased with it that I contacted her directly with additional questions. From the moment I spoke with Susie, I knew she would make an amazing business coach and mentor. I immediately made the investment and signed up for her professional coaching program. It's only been a couple of months and my business has more than doubled in size. Using Susie's advice, I saw instant results! I now have a team of consultants and more bookings on my calendar than ever. While my company has tons of training, I found it to be too overwhelming and, frankly, not as useful as the guidance I've received from Susie. Susie has taught me how to book shows, how to have conversations about my business, and how to train new consultants. She breaks everything down and makes it so simple, anyone can achieve success by following her formula! If you are in the direct sales business and are looking to grow your business, Susie's coaching program is for you! Sign up...you'll not be disappointed!

Tara Murray, Star Stylist, Stella & Dot

Taking a class with Susie Nelson is life and business changing. Fantastic presentations, personal attention, and everything you need to take your business to the next level. Susie has a way of taking the business and breaking it into easily duplicatable steps, and you can learn at your own pace. Highly recommend!!

Beth Millman, Independent petPro, pawTree

I was feeling overwhelmed with all the pieces of running my network marketing business. Taking Susie's training has helped me get organized and learn how to simplify the steps to my business. I now feel confident to train others on my team how to keep it simple using the skills of inviting, booking, follow-up and training! Such practical skills, thanks Susie!

Heather Gall, Young Living Essential Oils

Susie Nelson's has been one of the best mentor/ teachers I have ever had. Her 8 week course has had a huge impact on my mindset about my Direct sales business. I now see myself sharing an opportunity with women not bugging them. Tremendous value! Susie's experience and honest opinions has you feeling a true connection immediately.
I love sharing in the community with other DM consultant and the feeling of support is vital in this business. I will always recommend Susie Nelson, she's the real deal. My sincerest gratitude for your wisdom.

Kristine Dutra, Ruby Ribbon

Taking a leap of faith and jumping heart-first into one of Susie Nelson's trainings and one-on-one coaching has been the best thing I have done for myself and my business so far! Susie is a mecca of experience in the Direct Selling World and she takes her experience and helps make it applicable to my specific business and my expertise. Her feedback and challenges to me have really made me take a close, hard look at myself and my business and I will be soaring! Thanks Susie!!

Sharon Prince, BeautiControl

I met Susie 2 years ago. A novice to the industry, she is exactly what I needed. Kind yet tells you what you NEED to hear. Firm yet always encouraging. Her information is clear, smart, doable, logical. In short, if YOU DESIDE to push through your own fears and do exactly what she tells you to do, you WILL succeed!! Excited, frustrated, impatient, happy, hopeful, not sure, positive. Do these emotions feel familiar? Susie helps you work through all of them!! Susie is and will always be the coach who believes in you more than you believe in yourself. She is smart so you be smart. Invest in yourself and hire Susie. It is the best decision I ever made! Thank you Susie I am honored to be mentored by you and be your friend.

Mary Ann Metcalf, Melaleuca

I have been really blessed to have known Susie Nelson for nearly 20 years now. We worked together in a former business where she became my mentor and dear friend. Last year, I reconnected with her to utilize her business coaching services to help me with my new business. From our very first consultation, she skillfully guided me to really focus on what I could work on each week to make my business thrive. I was making myself stress out over all the things I wasn't doing with this business; but her uncanny ability to attentively listen to my specific situation and then suggest some very simple potential possibilities totally turned me around! I honestly believe breaking my overwhelming list of 'things to do' down into manageable daily or weekly tasks was most helpful. Taking her advice, I advanced my business within the first month of coaching. Most of us have some pretty amazing skills; but when you add the remarkable talents of a coach like Susie to keep you focused—you just can't help but soar to new heights! I would recommend Susie to anyone I know who is looking to gain that extra competitive edge to succeed in whatever business they are in—she is simply exceptional!

LindaRobinson, Melaleuca

Susie's "Booking Blitz" came at the perfect time. I had a lot of anxiety about calling people to book parties. It was *way* out of my comfort zone! Susie spoon fed us. She told us exactly what we needed to know--what to say, what not to say, when to say it and why. She eagerly answered questions and, in her calm, soothing manner, she instilled a confidence in those of us participating in the Blitz. At the end of the Blitz, I had booked 3 parties! And the next morning I booked 1 more! Susie's methods work! It was time well spent and I intend to do it again every chance I get.

Brenda Redfern, Premier Designs

Susie's free 4 day training for "8 Weeks to Your Promotion" is so funn of actionable information that I can use to boost my personal business AND coach my personal team to success! This is THE BEST training you should invest your time in! I guarantee you will be taking notes and actually USING them.

Jessica Davison, Paparrazzi

When I first met Susie I would have never imagined earning a six figure income in sales. Susie gives you the keys to success and then shows you how to be consistent in your results by time proven methods and some outside of the box ideas as well. She is an outstanding trainer and coach who is able to break down the steps and help you to move from mediocrity into excellence in your career and business.

Joellen Sutterfield, former Sr. Exec. Sales Manager, Weekenders USA

Before I started working with Susie I was just going along for the ride with my business. Susie helped me become intentional in everything I do, from booking to sponsoring to hostess coaching. Everything I do is now done with intent to grow my business. In less than a year I have doubled the size of my organization and am about to promote my first leader. With Susie's help, i have also been able to concur my crippling fear of the phone and am able to help my teammates get over their fears as well. I am looking to promote once again this year and know that it because of Susie's strategies and guidance that it is possible.

Helene Leonard, Director, ThirtyOne Gifts

8 Weeks to Your Promotion in Your Home Party Business

How to Rapidly Qualify for a Promotion, and Get Paid at Title Every Single Month

© 2014 Susie Nelson

All rights reserved. No portion of this book may be reproduced, stored in a retrieval system, or transmitted in any form or by any means - electronic, mechanical, photocopy, recording, scanning, or other, - except for brief quotations in critical reviews or articles, without the prior written permission of Susie Nelson or the publisher.

Limit of Liability / Disclaimer of Warranty: While the publisher and author have used their best efforts in preparing this book, they make no representations or warranties regarding the accuracy or completeness of the contents of this book. The publisher and author specifically disclaim any implied warranties of merchantability or fitness for a particular purpose and make no guarantees whatsoever that you will achieve any particular result. Any case studies that are presented herein do no necessarily represent what you should expect to achieve, since business success depends on a variety of factors. We believe all case studies and results presented herein are true and accurate, but we have not audited the results. The advice and strategies contained in this book may not even be suitable for your situation, and you should consult your own advisors as appropriate. The published and the author shall not be held liable for any loss of profit or any other commercial damages, including but not limited to special, incidental, consequential, or other damages. The fact that an organization or website is referred to in this work as a citation and/or a potential source of information does not mean that the publisher or author endorses the information the organization or website may provide or the recommendations it may make.

Earnings Disclaimer: The author does not believe in get rich programs — all human progress and accomplishment takes hard work. As stipulated by law, we cannot and do not make any guarantees about your ability to get results or earn any money with our ideas, information, tools or strategies. After all, it takes hard work to succeed in any type of business. In fact, it takes hard work to succeed at ANYTHING in life — try learning to play the piano without putting in any work, and see how that goes! your results in life are up to you and the amount of effort and resources that you are willing to put into succeeding. Nothing in this book is a promise or guarantee of results or future earnings, and we do not offer any legal, medical, tax or other professional advice. Any financial numbers referenced here, or on any of our sites, are simply estimates or projections and should not be considered exact, actual or as a promise of potential earnings — all numbers are illustrative only. In fact, the average person who purchases this book and other programs never finishes the book, never puts the work into implementing the strategies taught, and therefore achieves little to no results.

Copyright © 2014 Susie Nelson
All rights reserved.
ISBN-13: 978-1500661991
ISBN-10: 1500661996

Dedicated to all of the off-spring managers I promoted directly, indirectly, or had the honor of training at my sales meetings in my former company. I learned a tremendous amount from each of you during that journey - thank you.

My direct off-spring managers:

Anne Nelson
Becka Thompson
Jean Taylor
Joellen Sutterfield
Paulette Bullinger
Geri Nichols
Pat Tobin
Jackie Gabbert
Becky Black
Marie Sestile
Amy Welle
Carla Brees
Jane McCoy
Kathleen Hunter
Julie Walker
Linda Robinson

2nd Level Managers (had to promote out within one year of their Sr. Manager promoting from my unit):
Donna Versola
Beth White
Kathleen Rhodes (honorable mention - she promoted at month 13)

My incredible friend I met through the business. She attended my training and promoted to management from another unit:
Wanda Manley

TABLE OF CONTENTS

Forward - by Megan Milar

If you are holding this book in your hands, then you are taking the *best* next step for your promotion.

I had the pleasure of meeting Susie Nelson in late December 2013. I was aware of her training program and was hoping she would come to Ohio. Almost a year after developing a women's accessories brand, Arova, I was leaning toward launching into the home party industry. I felt like I was treading into a black hole because I had no personal or professional experience in that industry. And what an immense and complicated industry it is with many caveats and a stream of new and dying companies! I knew I could only venture down that road with the expertise of someone from the "inside". I reached out to Susie and a week later we were meeting in a hotel conference room in Beckley, WV one snowy morning. The humanitarian mission of our brand intrigued her and I was thoroughly impressed with her knowledge and experience in the home party industry. Not only had she successfully built a sales team and was a top producer in that company for 19 years, but she had also worked the corporate side of two other start-up brands. I knew right then she was the one person I needed to launch Arova (plus her bubbly personality is addictive)!

Over the next several months we worked together by phone and in person. We created the foundation for our launch including compensation plans, career path, marketing plans, training materials, reorders processes, and a fundraising program. Susie continued to impress us with her vast knowledge of the existing home party companies and her creative problem solving approach. We even worked several events together where I was able to see her in action. She really takes a sincere interest in getting to know people and by doing so is able to make strong connections for a brand.

Also during this time, I had the pleasure of attending two of her training programs. One was online and the other was in-person. I was most impressed with her subtle approach that brings in big results. Her training materials are all written in an easy step-by-step guide with specific wording. She also developed several different training guides that our consultants receive in their starter kit. They are frequently commenting on how they go back and reference those materials regularly!

In this busy life, we must all make choices on how to spend our time. I know there is a lot of information available on how to succeed in home party sales, but I can promise you *this is the one* to read! Susie will guide you right to your next promotion. The practical information included you can apply today. Susie has developed these systems through her own successes and failures. We are blessed that she has a passion for coaching others and is willing to share her insights to help you go straight to the top!

Megan Milar
Founder/CEO
www.arovastudio.com

Why I Wrote This Book

I saw it happen again just a few weeks ago. A woman, who shall remain nameless, "tried" to achieve a promotion…and failed. It truly breaks my heart.

This woman's experience could have been different.

She's not one of my coaching students - and I've learned over the years that providing people with free coaching and advice is a complete waste of time. Most only pay attention and implement your advice when they have some "skin in the game."

I know. Many of the consultants who join home party or network marketing businesses don't start to build a business, per se.

They want a little extra cash, or they want to spend a couple nights a week with adults, or they love a company's products and want a discount. So they think about their business from "party-to-party" rather than visualizing themselves building an organization…then an empire.

For me, being part of a home party business was always about building a business. Once I "caught the vision" and looked at the possibilities, I was determined to earn the highest possible commissions that were dangling out there for me.

I take a very strategic and systematic approach to this business. I'm a numbers geek - so I always let the numbers and data do the talking.

I had the opportunity to coach dozens as they prepared for qualification in my former company - and I learned a lot from that experience. (And now, you get to benefit from that, too.)

I've reviewed compensation plans of many different companies.

In most of those plans - and this may ruffle a few feathers when I say this - earning a promotion really isn't difficult. You might "think" it's hard (and we have to change that thinking) but when you really break down the numbers - it's not.

Plus, compared to the corporate world — where to even think about earning a promotion, a position has to be available, and you often have to complete interviews and be awarded the job by beating out hundreds of candidates — in our home party world the opportunity to earn your first, or next, promotion is just dangling out there for anyone who wants to do the work.

So what are you waiting for?

I wrote this book (and developed a full step-by-step training course) to be your coach and mentor so you are well prepared to enter qualification, you breeze through qualification, easily earn a promotion (stress-free!), and you create so much momentum that you get paid at title every single month.

I've broken it down into a step-by-step process. Complete step one. Check. Complete step two. Check.

Follow this roadmap and before you know it - you've earned a promotion.

How does that sound to you?

Do or Do Not.
There is No "Try"

- Yoda

My Story (or at least some of it)

If you've attended any of my free training classes, you've probably heard me share the story of my rocky start in direct sales.

After two failed attempts at selling activewear (the first company was shut down by the bank; the second ceased operations after one short year), I was extremely hesitant when my future sponsor sent me information about another new company she had discovered called Weekenders USA.

I literally threw the envelope on the junk mail pile on the corner of my desk, and ignored the packet for at least three or four months.

Here's something I've never shared before.

After the second company closed its doors, I decided I would launch my own screen-printed activewear business.

I attended a screen printing course down in Kansas; invested in a 4-color printer, screens, ink, and an inventory of t-shirts and sweatshirts; and hired the graphics guy from the plastics manufacturing firm where I worked to create my initial designs.

I even managed to sell a few!

But since I was working mega hours in my engineering job, that meant doing the screen printing to fill orders in the wee hours of the night…in my garage that wasn't heated…in the middle of the winter.

I decided to take a closer look at the information about Weekenders as a way of offering more options to my customers, since I had a limited number of my screen printed designs in my collection.

So I called up Sharon (the woman from the previous two companies who sent me the information) and arranged to meet with her on my next trip to the Twin Cities (I was living in Sioux Falls, SD at the time - so it was a 5 hour drive.)

Sharon had the clothes hanging around the living room from her drapery rods. Frankly, they didn't look very good. But I was impressed by the quality of the product, and by the outfit Sharon was wearing.

She sent me home with an application and sample order form. I sent it off to Weekenders, along with $600 for my new kit - and never heard from Sharon again. (Apparently she had been offered a new opportunity and decided to quit!)

My kit included a very nice training manual (that I never read), and a video tape that showed how to do a presentation (but I didn't own a VCR at the time, so I never watched it).

So as I held some of my open houses to show my own screen printing collection, I literally had the box in the corner in my bedroom, and I explained that there were some nice mix-n-match knits in it, in case they wanted to take a look.

In Weekenders, consultants started their businesses at a 25% discount ("Discount" because we strictly paid the company what we owed them for the wholesale purchase of the clothing; consultants absorbed the cost of the hostess rewards.). Your discount level increased, based on your cumulative lifetime sales. At $1000, it went to 30%; $3000 it went to 35%; and once you reached $5000+ in lifetime sales, you were at the full 40% discount and stayed there, as long as you remained active.

Most consultants achieved the 40% commission level in three-to-six weeks.

With my "hey, check out the stuff in that box" approach, it took me 8 months.

I started to receive a newsletter in the mail from my Sales Manager, Nancy. Browsing through it (I still wasn't highly engaged) I noticed the recognition immediately. The "presentation totals" and "monthly sales totals" definitely caught my attention.

I'll never forget the day I called her up and said, "My name is Susie Nelson - and I'm in your unit. I noticed that you're hosting a holiday party next weekend. If I drive up to the cities to attend it, would you be willing to show me one of these 'presentation things' I keep reading about in your newsletter?"

Fortunately, she put that together for me the Monday after the holiday party. I was blown away by it. It was clever, it kept the guests entertained, and most of all, that presentation was designed to produce sales, bookings and prospects (although I wasn't ready to think about prospects - at least not yet!).

I went home and started booking parties and started learning how to continually increase sales and bookings.

That's when Nancy offered an incentive for a big sample bag. It would hold all of my samples perfectly, and I decided…with five days left in the incentive…to earn that bag. (Nothing like waiting until the last minute!)

I had a party booked, so I approached my hostess, Carol, about looking at the business - and she agreed. We met for coffee at her home, and she seemed genuinely interested, but said she needed to think about it.

Now there were three days left in the incentive.

I made an appointment to return in two days, and showed up at Carol's door, right on time.

She opened the door and said, "You're a pushy, awful person. You're pushing me to do this, and I don't appreciate it. Don't bother me again."

And she shut the door.

I was devastated. I went home and cried because I couldn't figure out what I had done to get such a visceral reaction.

I went out and purchased a big tote bag later that afternoon, and vowed never to put myself in a situation where wanting to earn a "stupid sample bag" could possibly expose me to more nasty women, like Carol.

And I didn't talk to anyone about the business...for the next year.

By the way - a couple years later I learned that Carol's boyfriend had been arrested for a DUI the night before I knocked on her door - and she had been up all night trying to get him out of jail.

I was definitely in the wrong place...at the wrong time!

Fortunately, a year later, I had an amazing hostess named Gail who, after telling me two or three times that she was interested in the business (and I was basically ignoring those comments), called me and said, "Susie, I'm ready to start with Weekenders, and I have two people who also want to sign. Please get over here with an application."

That's how I got back on the sponsoring track…and eventually mastered my sponsoring skills.

As you can see…my business got off to a "less-than-stellar" start.

I sponsored Gail on January 2nd, 1991.

By the time I went to the company's National Conference in early March, I was a team leader (that title was earned when you sponsored your 3rd consultant, and started earning commissions on your team).

At that conference, **I caught the vision**. I realized that through the crazy, twisted path I had taken into the home party world; I had stumbled into a solid business opportunity.

One of my biggest observations was the diversity of the women who had achieved management to-date. One (my Sr. Manager) had won beauty contests and was married to a small animal veterinarian. Another was a single Mom who quit her job as a paralegal and was able to stay home with her young son, thanks to her new business. Another was bouncing across the stage, excited and loaded with energy because she was already earning more money than she ever imagined possible - even though her husband didn't want her holding parties on weekends.

It was a diverse, incredible group. I was truly inspired hearing their stories.

I left that conference saying to myself, "If they can do it, I believe I can, too."

On the plane ride home, I made a **commitment** to focus and build my business to the management level as quickly as possible.

Meeting the requirements:

In order to enter qualification for management, I had to meet these requirements:

- Be a Fashion Coordinator for at least one year.

- Have personal retail sales of at least $9000+ in the 6 months prior to entering qualification.

- Directly sponsor at least 12 active Fashion Coordinators.

  - At least 8 had to be with Weekenders for over one month.

  - 3 had to be at a 40% discount (i.e. $5000+ in cumulative lifetime sales)

  - Two of my directly sponsored Fashion Coordinators had to personally sponsor at least one Fashion Coordinator (note: These "2nd level" Coordinators did not become part of your future unit. My team members had sponsored 8 Fashion Coordinators when I entered qualification.)

- Six must have retail sales of at least $1500 each during the 3 months prior to entering qualification.

Qualification was a 3 month period:

During that time-frame, with the help of your team, you had to build to a unit of at least 20 active Fashion Coordinators, and achieve wholesale production of at least $15,000 (retail of approximately $25,000) total during the 3 months. My personal sales did not count in that total.

I'm very proud to share that we sailed through qualification. My team and I entered qualification on September 1st, completed the requirements by the first week of November, and I earned a promotion to the Sales Manager level with a unit of 23 Fashion Coordinators on December 1st that same year.

But I didn't stop there.

I kept building. I focused on developing leaders from day one, and it really paid off, when it came to building my business to the very highest level offered in the company.

In its first full year, my unit achieved $293,000 in sales (remember - my sales didn't count). And the following year, when my company introduced its first "Circle of Excellence" trip - a week in Hawaii - for achieving $1 Million+ in unit sales, I was one of only six managers who earned the trip.

That was just the beginning.

I replaced my engineering income in my second year as a manager by building my commissions to six figures (and maintaining that level for 11 years straight).

(Go to: SusieNelson-Training.com/proof to see my 1099s.)

I earned trips to amazing places around the world - Hong Kong, Bali, Turkey, Greece, Paris, Spain, to name a few of my favorites.

My organization was always in the top 10% in the country (and most of the time, in the top 5%) for annual sales.

I believe leaders promote leaders - and that was always my focus.

I was the second manager in the company to promote to National Sales Manager - the highest level offered at the time. This was achieved by promoting out 10 (or more) offspring units. Only six managers in the U.S. company ever achieved the National Manager title.

I also promoted the most managers of anyone in the U.S. company.

I learned an amazing amount by coaching and mentoring these incredible women through the qualification and promotion process.

That's what I'm sharing with you in this book.

I'm thrilled that you're focused on earning your first — or next — promotion.

Once you learn this strategic approach…you will be equipped to build exponential growth in your organization.

When this happens, it's exciting, challenging, exhilarating, and often life-altering.

As Ralph Waldo Emerson said, "Life is a journey, not a destination." Get ready for an amazing experience.

It's all right to have butterflies in your stomach.

Just get them to fly in formation.

- Dr. Rob Gilbert

A Note About the Examples in this Book

Many of the strategies I'll be explaining are easier to understand with specific examples.

I decided to use one specific company's compensation plan to make my examples more clear.

So you can follow along (whether this is your plan or not), here's the details.

To promote to Sr. Consultant, all you need to do is:

- Sponsor at least 2 personally enrolled, qualified consultants.

You'll earn 2% commissions on their personal sales volume.

Here's its requirements to promote to a Director:

- Personally sponsor at least four qualified consultants (a consultant is "qualified" when she achieves $1000 in personal sales volume).
- Submit $1000 in personal volume every month.
- Minimum team sales (your volume plus Generation 0* volume) of $4000 per month.
- The promotion occurs the month following your qualification month.

* Generation 0 is all consultants in your downline, down to and including the next director.

In this plan, a director can earn a one-time promotion bonus of $1000 when she and her team meet all of the Director requirements for the first 3 consecutive months following the qualification month. (Sounds like a great perk to me - and I want you to earn any bonus your company puts out there for you.)

(Don't worry - if this plan doesn't look familiar - I'll be teaching you how to evaluate the requirements for your compensation plan.)

Part I: Key Concepts

Before I can dive into the the strategies and implementation plan for earning a promotion in the next 8 weeks — I have to explain some key business concepts.

Where are you at in your business?

Consultants typically fall into one of these categories when it comes to earning a promotion:

1) You're a new consultant in your company. You've been with it for less than a year, but despite your short tenure, you see the "big picture" and you're ready to earn a promotion.

Congratulations.

Don't let anything (or anyone!) slow you down.

Focus. Learn the "essential skills" that I'll be explaining later, and take massive action.

You can build - to the top - as quickly as you choose - and you deserve it!

2) You've been in the business for more than a year - possibly two years, three years, or even longer - and haven't earned your first promotion.

If this is you - what's up?

What I normally find in this scenario is consultants haven't mastered their booking skills yet. As a result, they don't sponsor many new team members (and if they do, it is usually "by accident"). More about this later.

Or, they think earning a promotion will be "difficult" or "a lot of work."

Worse yet - some are simply afraid. Whether they fear asking prospects to look at the business, or they fear they will sponsor people who won't succeed - something is stopping them from reaching out to their prospects.

I want to help you move past your self-imposed barriers. Often some "friendly accountability" really helps you to stay focused, and push through any fears or perceived obstacles.

3) You've earned a promotion - but you rarely get paid at title.

Usually this happens when a consultant barely makes it through qualification - and then stops doing the business building activities that she did to earn the promotion in the first place.

I challenge you to mentally "put yourself back in qualification."

As you go through this book, I believe you'll see a new approach - an approach that will result in building a strong foundation for your business, and a way to build the momentum to create exponential growth.

When my coaching students earn their first promotion - I immediately challenge them to double their organization. I want them to capitalize on the momentum they've started to create and keep right on going.

It's time for you to get back in the game.

4) You've earned a promotion - and for whatever reason, you didn't maintain it.

Ouch.

Sometimes life circumstances get in the way - an illnesses or death of a family member, for example.

The beauty of our business model is that you can simply start over after dealing with those difficult experiences.

But if you're in the much more common category - that you didn't maintain your promotion because your team stopped producing, or team members left your business for another company, or you didn't personally produce the monthly sales requirement - I've got great news for you.

It's time to start fresh.

You actually have a huge advantage. You've learned a lot from that previous experience.

Your past does not have to equal your future. The strategies and the implementation plan I'll be sharing in later sections of this book will help you approach your business (and your NEXT promotion) differently.

This time around, you'll build such a strong foundation that your business can move to exponential growth in a very short period of time.

I'm very happy that you're ready to earn another promotion. Let's make sure you approach it "the right" way the second time around.

5) You've earned a promotion - and now your future promotions depend on building leaders within your organization.

Get ready for rapid expansion!

The best, and smartest way to build your business — and your income — is to start building leaders.

Lots of them.

Leaders build leaders. That's how you'll earn six figures (or higher), and you'll do so while helping and empowering others.

Unfortunately, this is often where businesses "plateau."

Making the shift from focusing on your personal business - to training, coaching and mentoring others - often becomes a huge road block.

Although leadership and coaching skills are beyond the scope of this book, I encourage you to use the step-by-step planning this book will take you through as your guide for developing leaders.

(Note: The full "8 Weeks to Your Promotion" Course has an entire section dedicated to leaders promoting leaders. One of the biggest mistakes leaders make is focusing on the wrong people. That is so frustrating, and it sucks away all of your energy and valuable time. More about that later.)

Many of life's failures are people who did not realize how close they were to success when they gave up.

- Thomas Edison

There's Not a Good Reason to Build Your Business S-L-O-W-L-Y.

Hard as I try, I can't think of any good reason for you to build your home party or network marketing business s-l-o-w-l-y.

From the minute you sponsor your first team member - you are literally losing money every month if you aren't capturing the highest commissions available through your compensation structure.

I used this fact to keep myself highly motivated as I built my organization.

Here's what I did:

Each month, when I received my sales reports for my unit, and my off-spring units, I calculated (OK, yes I even kept a chart - I'm a numbers geek) the amount of commissions that I DIDN'T receive, because I wasn't - YET - at the highest level in the compensation structure.

As I promoted more and more managers, the amount I was leaving on the table each month became alarming. Perhaps an even better description would be highly irritating.

In my former company, once you achieved the National Manager title (by promoting at least 10 off-spring Managers) you were at the full 2% commissions on all of your off-spring managers' units. Several of my off-spring managers followed my lead, and also built Circle of Excellence (at least $650,000 per year) units. So the commissions I was missing out on started piling up.

By the time I promoted my ninth manager, I was missing out on several thousand dollars (or more) in senior manager commissions each month.

I stayed focused and continued building leaders - both because I love to help others succeed, and because I deserve to earn those additional commissions.

You do, too.

The faster you move up your compensation structure, the faster you build your income AND stop missing out on commissions that are available for you.

Let me give you an example.

Using my example compensation plan, at the Sr. Consultant level you earn 2% overrides on any personally enrolled, qualified consultant.

Let's say those two consultants follow my "Success Formula" (more about that later) and their sales are $2000 per month each, for total team sales of $4000.

At the Sr. Consultant level, you will earn an override of $80.

That's nice. It can pay the water bill, or treat the family to dinner and a movie.

But what if you were at the top?

What if you hit the National Executive Director level?

On those same two consultants - you would now earn a 9% override (versus 2%) for a total of $360. A difference of $280 (not to mention the additional overrides you'll earn on a boatload of other consultants in your downline).

Let me take it one step further.

Let's say that you just linger at that Sr. Consultant level for a couple years.

With my example, as a Sr. Consultant earning just 2%, you'll earn overrides of $1920 during that two year period.

But you will "walk away" from $6720 in commissions simply because you haven't earned promotions.

Ouch.

I know - you're going to start driving yourself a little crazy, like I did - each month, too! Good! Let it motivate you and keep you focused.

What Compensation Plans are Designed to Accomplish.

There are certainly a lot of different compensation plans, and every company's plan has its own unique twists.

A home party company has to consider a lot of factors when developing its plan — especially when it comes to the financial impact paying out full commissions (as it grows) will have on its bottom line.

The intention of the compensation or career plan is to encourage and reward consultants for helping increase the company's sales.

Most compensation plans have five key factors:

1) Personal Sales Requirement

This is an amount a leader must personally sell each month in order to be paid at title.

(More about this number when I teach you my "Success Formula" in a later section.)

2) Personal Sponsoring Requirement

Obviously building a solid team and organization starts with personal sponsorships.

Learning the skill (and it is just that - a skill) of sponsoring new consultants is a valuable investment. It enables you to build the foundation of your organization.

This is an area where many leaders make a huge mistake. I'll tell you about it in a later section.

3) Team Sales Requirement

It doesn't matter how many new consultants you sponsor. If they don't schedule parties consistently, your team is going nowhere fast.

Any percent of $0 in team sales = $0 commissions or overrides.

Write down and study what I'm about to say next.

The amount your team sells each month is a reflection of what you teach them and in many respects "expect" them to do.

Sure - there's always going to be a percentage who won't break away from their cell phones or switch off their favorite reality TV show to take the actions that can change their circumstances and pad their pocketbooks.

But most of the people who come into our businesses want to be successful. They just don't always know how to do it.

I'll be going into my rant about this in a future section - but I want you to start thinking about how you plan to coach and mentor your personally sponsored team members.

In turn, think about how you will teach, and expect, your team members to coach and mentor team members they sponsor - and so on.

It all begins with you.

4) Team Sponsoring Requirement

Many plans don't have this requirement in the first couple promotion levels.

But if you want to create exponential growth in your organization, teaching your team members how to sponsor - and how to do it well - is a key ingredient.

When I work with my private coaching students - I teach them a technique for teaching their team members to sponsor that takes an investment of a few hours of their time up front.

But once their team members learn to sponsor - and realize it can be a fun and eventually lucrative investment in their business - these consultants are on the fast track to being your future leaders.

5) Developing and promoting leaders.

One of my mentors, the President of my former company, always said, "They're either moving up or they're moving out."

Now, more than ever, I believe this to be true.

In my playbook, this business is all about building people and developing leaders.

That happens when they learn Steps 1-through-4: Personal Sales, Personal Sponsoring, developing Team Sales, and teaching their Team to Sponsor.

Now you might be saying, "This is obvious - that's how you build your organization," but you'd be surprised how easily consultants get sucked off course.

That's why I'm going to share my secrets to soaring through your qualification and promotion in the next section.

Rather than becoming discouraged…consider that obstacles tell you what to do next."
- Kay Leigh Hagan

The Secret to Building Your Business Quickly - and Creating Exponential Growth:

Get ready for it. Because I'm going to share a huge secret. Learn this and continually remind yourself of this and your business will explode.

The secret is: **Balance.**

What I mean by Balance is that you dedicate an equal amount of time to the four activities that build your business: personal sales, personal sponsoring, team sales and team sponsoring.

It also doesn't matter how many hours you have per week to invest in your business. Those hours simply need to be spread - as evenly as possible - across these four activities.

(For a helpful tracking form to manage your hours each week go to: 8WeekstoYourPromotion.com/balance)

That might seem obviously - yet it is the way most consultants get side-tracked.

Let me give you some examples.

Let's say consultant A, who wants to build her organization, has 12 hours per week that she can dedicate to her business, and she books 2 or 3 shows per week.

Consultant A loves the profits she earns from her parties.

The problem: Consultant A doesn't have much very much time left to meet with prospects, train new consultants, and teach them how to sponsor.

If she does achieve a promotion, Consultant A will probably be completing the majority of her team sales requirement herself. That's a lot of pressure each month.

Next, meet Consultant B. She is a sponsoring machine. She loves meeting people and connects with prospects everywhere she goes (after all - prospects are everywhere!).

The problem: No one is doing any selling.

This consultant will have a huge team that is barely staying active.

Consultant C built her organization, then stopped doing very much of her personal business.

Fortunately she has some strong sellers on her team, so her team is meeting their sales requirement each month.

But here's the problem. Since Consultant C doesn't achieve her personal sales requirement - she rarely gets paid at title.

(This is the leader who goes into that vicious and stressful cycle of meeting her numbers strictly when she is down to the wire of maintaining her organization and title. Often in 3 months cycles. This is not a fun, or lucrative way to run a business.)

Consultant D has focused on helping everyone sponsor. She will have team members moving into qualification.

The problem is - as those team members promote, Consultant D hasn't built a strong foundation for her organization. Depending on the plan, as she promotes leaders, she is in danger of losing her own title if she doesn't "rebuild." (A word that I HATE, based on my experience with my former company!)

Let me tell you about one of my off-spring managers - a woman named Anne.

She is bright, enthusiastic, and an incredible teacher and coach.

Anne gave birth to her second child the month she entered qualification. Obviously we knew this was going to happen! And she wasn't going to let this life event slow down her business.

Anne and I had mapped out her strategic plan for achieving her qualification - despite having a newborn and her other busy toddler at home.

One day I got a call from her husband. He was concerned because he felt Anne was booking too many parties herself - and he was right. She had booked a lot more parties than we discussed.

So I sat down with Anne - we reviewed her plan - and she gave away some of her parties (the ones with hostesses who had already held two or three parties in the past) to her very best team members, and re-allocated her time.

(Note: At the time, in my former company, our personal sales did not count towards our promotion sales requirements. So during qualification, every party you personally booked needed to be for sponsoring new consultants, or for helping a new consultant launch her business. Post promotion, our personal sales also did not count in our team sales. Eventually the company made a change to allow a small portion - about 10% of the overall requirement - to count during the qualification period.)

Every week, as you look at what is happening with your business while you prepare to enter qualification - it's important to evaluate how your time is being used for each of the four activities - and to dedicate a portion of your time to each.

Lather, Rinse, Repeat

To me, the home party business should operate like a well-oiled machine. I implement systems and processes for everything - and my home party business was no exception.

When you approach the business as a process - you can "optimize" it.

Think about that famous clip from "I Love Lucy" where she and Ethel go to work in the chocolate factory? (If you haven't seen it, google "Lucy in the chocolate factory.) Needless to say, it's a process that is out of control.

That's what happens when your business isn't balanced, and hasn't been fine-tuned.

Instead, think "assembly line" - like a car manufacturing plant. You want this to be a simple process that you can fine-tune, and (as the woman says at the end of the "I Love Lucy" clip) - speed up.

Here's the process:

- **Network** (this includes making a list of your connections, if you're a new consultant).
- **Get people excited about your products.**
- Once they're excited about the products, explain your hostess rewards and **book parties!**
- **Coach your hostesses extremely well** (this is also the beginning of the sponsoring process).

- **Do an effective (and well-rehearsed) presentation** at your party that results in high sales, several future bookings, and business prospects.

- **Meet with your prospects to share information about your business**.

- **Sponsor some - and train them extremely well.**

- Repeat.

It's a very simple business - and simple process.

What I learned is that consultants who don't follow the process - in order - make the business more difficult - and often get frustrated. They also slow down their business growth tremendously.

For example, (and this is especially true if your company is not well known yet), asking someone to book a show without first showing them some samples often results in a party with low attendance and low sales. The hostess just isn't excited or engaged. She is simply doing the party to help a friend.

Consultants who choose to "wing it" rather than use a well-planned and practiced presentation, often struggle with low sales, book very few parties from their parties, and rarely connect with a prospect.

The consultant who doesn't ask every customer to take a look at her business information spends way too much time trying to connect with prospects via phone or other mediums post party.

And so on…and so on…

(In the "8 Weeks to Your Promotion Course," I will teach you how to use this simple "Lather-Rinse-Repeat" formula to coach your team members and identify where they are getting stuck. It works extremely well!)

Keep the business simple, and repeatable. Period.

(Wo)Men are born to succeed, not fail.

- Henry David Thoreau

You Need the Right Mindset

Anyone can take focused action and eventually achieve a promotion in the home party world. Anyone.

You don't need a college degree or a high school diploma; it doesn't matter what you look like; it doesn't matter how long you've been "on the job," like it does in the corporate world.

But there's one thing that can help you build your business faster and stronger…

…having the right mindset.

There are several areas about "mindset" I need to discuss.

1) *Do you absolutely believe you are offering an incredible opportunity that can have a strong, positive impact on a person's life?*

This is big.

Make a list.

Start with all the attributes about your company.

What do you love about your company leaders? Write down ten things that you appreciate about your leaders and their vision for the future of the company.

Next - what about your products? How do they help people? Why do people need them?

Of course, we also need to talk about your business opportunity.

How can starting a business with your company and being part of your team be an incredible opportunity - possibly life-changing?

Obviously the extra income can help people tremendously and can give consultants a tool to achieve many of their dreams.

Getting out of debt, paying for college tuition, treating the family to a much-needed vacation, buying a new car, or being able to stay home with their children.

I'm sure you can add dozens of additional items to the "how can the added income help" list.

But don't stop there.

Perhaps it's the recognition. You will be amazed as you build your business and witness how being recognized for specific milestones and achievements can impact a person positively.

It might be the need to spend a couple nights per week with adults. I hear this a lot from stay-at-home and work-at-home Moms.

The business might help a person build their confidence. I've watched women whose knees were shaking, simply getting up to do a presentation - conquer that fear and build Million Dollar organizations.

Being part of your business might also provide a social outlet for some consultants. The person who is looking for a way to meet more women and make new friends. It certainly provides all of that.

For some, it might also be tax write-offs. Small businesses have many tax advantages over hourly or salaried employees.

But let's go further.

People like to be affiliated with winners. That's you. They want to be part of a productive team and a growing team.

They are fortunate to be part of YOUR team!

So I've briefly shared a few ideas with you to get you started. Now you make your list!

Put it away for a few hours - and then review your list.

It's possible there are a few things about your company that you don't "love." Companies are living, breathing entities that go through different phases. There will be some things that you love, and some that you wish were different.

Maybe they're struggling with some backorders, or maybe their consultant back office isn't the best...yet.

If there are areas where you have concerns - reach out to your sponsor, to your upline, to your corporate trainers - and discuss your concerns.

You need to be absolutely certain that the business opportunity you are offering others can change peoples' lives.

2) Building this business is all about helping others - it's not about you.

This is important - especially as you prepare for qualification - to keep the right perspective.

Over the past few months, working with private coaching students and hundreds of students enrolled in my training programs, I've heard a lot of examples where consultants put the focus on what they want, rather than focusing on what prospective customers, hostesses, and team members want.

Let me give you some examples.

The consultant who asks for bookings by saying, "Do you want to have a party for me?"

The consultant who is talking to a prospect and says, "I want you on my team."

The future leader who announces to her networking group that she "needs them to sign-up for parties because she's in her leader qualification period."

Don't misunderstand me here.

I believe you should set goals, see yourself earning a promotion, see yourself earning big commissions, and so on.

But when it comes to how you build your business, when you start connecting with your customers and prospects - you have to put your own goals into a "mental black box" and keep your focus on your prospects.

One of my private coaching students and I have been discussing ways for her to increase her sales at her shows.

Since we connect by phone, I asked her to take me through her presentation from beginning to end. I asked her to be specific. I wanted to know - what does she say, what does she pass out, what happens when you pass out your samples, etc. I needed to get a clear understanding of how her parties flow - and where we could make some changes to increase sales per party rapidly.

P a g e | 39

It became immediately obvious that the problem - one that will change her results dramatically and immediately if she spends time working on it - is that her focus was on her.

She was using phrases such as "I want to find a new home for a couple cases of X." She was also jumping to immediate conclusions about who would purchase - or who wouldn't - based on their answers to the questions on her "customer survey."

(By the way, if you've studied anything about the psychology of selling - and I recommend that you do - a survey that you hand out to guests at the beginning or anytime during your sales presentation needs to be structured and worded very carefully to support your sales. If not, it can hurt as much as it can help.)

Finally, during our discussion, to rattle her thinking - I had to use a curse word.

I specifically said, "In the big picture of this business - your customers, prospective hostesses, and potential team members don't give a S-&-%-@ (yes, you can fill in those blanks) what YOU want. They care about how your products or hosting a presentation or looking at your business will impact THEIR lives.

Sure - when we're first getting started - we reach out to our close connections - family, friends, neighbors. Many will host a party to help us out. But once that initial "help me start my business" phase has passed, you have to be clear about your intention.

3) Do you think it's easy or hard to earn a promotion?

Often consultants - especially those who've been in the business longer than a year, or have achieved a promotion in the past, but didn't maintain it - are slowed by thinking that this achievement is difficult.

If you think it will be a lot of work, or you think it will be hard to maintain - you will become a self-fulfilling prophecy.

In a future section of the book, I'll be helping you break down the qualification and title maintenance requirements into parts.

Once we do this, I'll ask you this question again.

4) Are you afraid of it?

Is earning a promotion and being among the leaders in your company the big scary monster that's ready to jump out of your closet?

I have to say - sometimes, based on observing some leaders in home party companies, I can understand where some fears might creep in.

The leader who is attached to her cell phone - answering texts and Facebook messages in the middle of dinner or secretly in the back of the movie theater.

Or the leader who has a "need" to make everything look difficult.

Let me assure you - you don't have to let this business take over your life. Nothing is life-or-death; nothing is rocket science.

In fact, you get to experience "on-the-job training" because you don't have to know leadership skills to achieve the promotion.

Most companies have great training programs for leaders AFTER they earn a promotion.

What do you think the responsibilities are as a leader in your company?

I suggest they are simply to coach and mentor consultants in your organization - so *those who choose* and *those who can be coached* - can achieve whatever level of success they desire.

Note the emphasis on "those who choose" and "those who can be coached."

You will attract a wide variety of people with interesting personalities into your business.

Some will become great friends; others not so much. That's life.

But as long as you can honestly look in the mirror and ask yourself, "Did I offer to help this person and reach out - just like I do for every other consultant on my team," if they don't want your help, that's their (poor) choice.

In the big picture of life - if someone starts with your business and chooses not to continue - you're not causing them any harm. Sample kit investments are so inexpensive that literally anyone can figure out how to start a home party business.

They don't have to take out a second mortgage, they don't have to apply for a small business loan.

In most companies, sample kits are the equivalent of dinner and a movie - or purchasing a new outfit.

And in most companies, the consultant is getting incredible products for that extremely small investment.

So I have to ask: What's the worst that can possibly happen when you sponsor a consultant into your business?

Technically, if your company is affiliated with the DSA, they have an outrageously long period of time to return samples to the company, for a significant refund (I believe it's 90%) if it doesn't work out.

Those consultants could also have a sample sale, or give those wonderful products as gifts.

Literally - no harm is done.

So the last question I need to ask: **What if you earn a promotion - and decide it's just not what you want?**

You can simply "not" maintain your title - or officially resign from your leadership position - and let your upline take on the leadership responsibilities.

No biggie.

You gave it a try - and decided it wasn't for you. Onto the next adventure.

5) *Do you believe you deserve it?*

If you don't think you're worthy or don't believe you deserve to be a leader in your company - that's what we really need to work on.

I've met thousands of consultants in my history in the business - and I haven't met a single one that I didn't feel deserved to earn a promotion.

Just the fact that you're looking for a book - such as this - that can guide you through the process - already sets you apart from the pack.

Your sponsor, your company leaders, and I believe in you - possibly much more than you believe in yourself.

That's not OK with me.

This is your time to shine.

In the upcoming pages, I'm going to help you break down the requirements, develop an implementation plan, and help you prepare so you can earn your promotion - and keep right on building.

You deserve it.

Let's get started!

Everyone who got where he is has had to begin where he was.

- Robert Louis Stevenson

Part II: Preparing for Qualification

Now that I've reviewed the basic concepts - it's time to start preparing to enter your qualification or promotion period.

This is probably the most important part - *preparing* well.

What are your requirements?

Grab your compensation or career plan - including all definitions and rules - for the level you're working to achieve.

Record each of your requirements:

- Personal Sales
- Personal Sponsoring
- Team Sales
- Team Sponsoring
- Leader Promotions

(For those in my full "8 Weeks to Your Promotion Course" - you'll find a handout to use for this evaluation in the "students only" section of the website. For more information, go to: 8WeekstoYourPromotion.com/new-course)

Are there any requirements that you must achieve prior to the start of your promotion month?

(For example, in my former company, there was a list of "pre-qualification requirements" we had to meet, prior to starting our 3-month qualification period. We also had to write a letter to the

President of the company, requesting to start our qualification; and our Sales Manager also had to write a letter of recommendation.)

Do your requirements change after you've achieved your promotion?

If yes, again record it for each category:

- Personal Sales
- Personal Sponsoring
- Team Sales
- Team Sponsoring
- Leader Promotions

Are there any additional bonuses or incentives?

(For example, in the plan I'm using for my example, a new leader and their upline leader can earn bonuses when the new leader and her team achieve their promotion requirements for the immediate three months following the qualification month.)

I want you to know your promotion requirements inside-and-out. Review them several times, and if you have any questions - reach out to your upline or consultant support for clarification.

Your "Success Formula"

I wanted to find a simple way to make sure leaders weren't just barely making their numbers each month - and at the same time, provide an easy way to set expectations with their team members to position and prepare them for outrageous success.

That's why I developed my "Success Formula."

(For students in my "8 Weeks to Your Promotion" course - look for the "Success Formula" form to do this calculation for your business.)

Here's how it works.

First - you take your personal sales amount required to be paid at title - and double it.

(In my example compensation plan - the leader is required to sell $1000 per month. I would double that to $2000 in personal sales per month.)

Next, simply divide that new sales goal by your average sales per party.

Using my example:

Let's say you are averaging $500 per party. $2000 divided by $500 per party = 4 parties per month. That's easy!

Next - look at the first level to start earning sponsoring overrides.

In my example, it is Sr. Consultant and requires at least 2 personally enrolled, qualified team members.

That's your goal each month. Focus to sponsor (and train) two new consultants!

So in my example, the "Success Formula" would be:

Sell at least $2000 by booking and holding 4 parties per month, and sponsor at least 2 new consultants every month.

That's it!

But here's the part that's really important.

Teach everyone you sponsor to do the exact same thing.

Will they all do it? No. But if you focus on this and teach it - and talk about it - a lot - some will!

What you focus on is what you get in this business.

Your consultants want to be successful.

Imagine how fast your organization will grow when a significant number of your team members do this.

But it will only happen if you focus on it and teach it.

Let's review:

Your Success Formula (Write this down and calculate it.)

Your Monthly Personal Sales Requirement _____

x 2 = _____(A)

Calculate the number of parties or shows you need to complete to achieve these sales:

(A) divided by your average sales per party = _____ parties per month.

Sponsor _____ New Consultants Per Month

And...

Teach Every Single Consultant in Your Team to Do The Same Thing!

It's time to start living the life you've imagined.

- Henry James

Creating Your Strategic Plan

Remember - this is all about: **BALANCE**

As we go through this section, I'm going to be asking you to calculate a few simple numbers. These are important numbers. This is the information a "business person" needs to monitor as they build a strong business.

If numbers "aren't your thing," there is no need to panic. Just stick with me as I walk you through it.

Let's start with where your business is at TODAY.

Pull out your list of promotion and title requirements (that you recorded in an earlier section).

Here's how we're going to create your strategic plan:

We're going to start with your personal business.

First, let's look at the number of parties you personally have to complete (per the success formula - we already went through that example and calculation) to easily achieve your personal monthly sales requirements.

Next, we'll determine the number of business prospects you need to connect with each week or each month to meet your personal sponsoring goal.

These will be very simple calculations. I want you to stick with me here as we walk through it - because this is how you will learn that your qualification can be a very easy process.

Next, we're going to look at your team sales requirement and break this down into the number of parties you and your team need to complete.

Finally, we'll look at team sponsoring and determine which of your team members are ready to sponsor (with some additional coaching and training from you).

To create this plan…we have to grind through the numbers.

(Plus - I will "tie in" your "Success Formula" so you can see how powerful it is to focus on it.)

(For those in the full "8 Weeks to Your Promotion" course - you have worksheets to take you through this information.)

Part One: Personal Sales

Based on your success formula, (where I recommend you double your personal sales requirement) how much do you personally need to sell per month: _____ (A)

In the previous section I explained that you need to divide that "doubled" sales goal by your average sales per party to determine the number of parties you need to complete.

Let's talk about average sales per party (this is an important number to monitor - both for your own sales and for each team member's sales - and I will be giving you an example later that will show you how to have a huge impact on your monthly team sales, based on what you'll learn from monitoring average sales per party).

What are your average sales per party? It's possible this information is available in you back office. But if this isn't available, you can easily calculate it.

Add up the total sales from your last 10 parties = _____.

Divide that number by 10 (parties) to get your average sales per party: _____. (B)

Next - Divide your personal sales needed per month (A) by your average sales per party (B) to get the number of parties you need to book each month in order to reach your personal sales goal (per my "Success Formula").

As I showed in my example, I would personally be focused on booking and holding 4 parties/shows per month. (I showed how to calculate this in the previous section.)

You can do that.

Part Two: Personal Sponsoring

Do you currently have a big prospect list?

Even if you already have the minimum number of personally sponsored consultants needed to qualify - why stop there?

I want you to think about this for a minute.

If you sponsor two new consultants per month (as I recommend in my example, with my "Success Formula") this will have a huge impact on your business. To me, this is building the "foundation" for your organization.

If every month, you have just two new personally sponsored consultants that you're helping launch their businesses - isn't that some nice team volume?

Let's say, per my example, that you have two consultants achieving their qualification requirement each month (it takes $1000 in sales to become "qualified"). That's $2000 in team sales.

Plus - and this is even more important - this is how you start building exponential growth in your organization.

It all starts with your personal sponsorships.

Pull out another piece of paper and start your prospect list.

If you've only got a couple names on that paper - you're not thinking big enough.

Let me help:

1) Every past hostess. She's a business prospect.

2) Every upcoming hostess (and hopefully you've got some bookings with NEW hostesses). She's a business prospect.

3) Every customer. She's a business prospect.

Does that make your prospect list quite a bit bigger?

Chances are you didn't ask every person on this list to take a closer look at your business in the past - am I right?

Even if you did - just because a person said "no thank you" previously doesn't mean circumstances haven't changed.

Remember - you're offering to share an opportunity that could literally change a person's life. Don't you want to spread that news?

Spend time making your prospect list including contact information. We'll talk about how to work that into your strategic plan in an upcoming section.

What will be important to monitor is the number of prospects you connect with in order to sponsor one new consultant onto your team.

Let me give you an example.

Let's say that at your party this week, there were three "hot prospects" who were anxious to learn more about your business.

You schedule appointments with each of them (or better yet - meet with all of them together as a group) to review your business information.

From those three prospect connection meetings (or one group meeting), you sponsor one new consultant onto your team.

So for now - we'll say that for every 3 connections you make, you'll sponsor at least one.

That is very helpful and powerful information to monitor. (The same is true for your team members who are sponsoring! Knowing how many prospects they have to meet in order to sponsor one new one is extremely helpful for coaching and training.)

Part Three: Team Sales Requirements

I want to start by calculating out the number of parties your overall team needs to complete to achieve the team sales requirement.

In my example, the team sales requirement is $4000 per month.

Using my $500 sales per party average (calculated earlier), $4000 divided by $500 = 8. So to achieve your team sales requirement, the team has to complete 8 parties.

There are also three things to consider.

a) Do a certain number of your team members need to reach sales milestones, such as being "qualified" or being "active"?

b) Do a certain number of team members need to sell a specific amount each month?

c) Do your personal sales count in your team sales requirement?

In the example I'm using, *at least* four of your consultants must be personally sponsored, active, and qualified. By definition, a "qualified consultant" has achieved cumulative lifetime sales of at least $1000.

Again, in my example, an "active consultant" must place an order of at least $200 every rolling 3 months.

Take a piece of paper and list, down the left side of the paper, all of your personally sponsored consultants, draw a line across, then list consultants sponsored by your team members.

Next, make a column for each requirement.

("8 Weeks to Your Promotion" students - there's a form and a video that walks you through it.)

In my example, it would be "qualified," "sales in the past two months (so I know if they have to order in the upcoming month to remain active)," "number of parties booked in (upcoming Month 1)," "number of parties booked in (upcoming Month 2)," "team members sponsored," and "number of prospects."

Go through each name on the list.

Is she qualified? Check.

How much have her sales been in the past two months? Fill in the number. Is it enough to be active? If yes - put a checkmark in that box.

How many parties does each consultant have booked in upcoming Month 1 and upcoming Month 2? (You might have to reach out and call each consultant to get that info if it's not available in your back office. More about that later.)

Record the numbers.

How many business prospects is each consultant currently working with?

Record those numbers, based on your conversations, too.

Next - total up each column at the bottom of the page.

By doing this, you will have a very clear, accurate snapshot of where your team is at, who needs some training and assistance, and whether or not you are realistically ready to enter qualification.

Compare your list to your requirements. What do you need to accomplish? Make the list.

Now that you've created this chart the first time - it will be easy to maintain from month to month.

This is simple, yet powerful information that can help you monitor and manage your team, and your organization, extremely well.

Let me give you an example. Let's say that you know you that you and your team need to have a total of 8 bookings on the calendar each month to meet your minimum requirements. Yet right now, the total shows you only have 6. Working with the team members who don't have any bookings, or only have 1 and want to book more, will help you get up to 8 (or more) bookings.

How will you feel going into your qualification month knowing, based on the number of bookings on both your calendar, and your team members calendars, you've got this covered?

Like I said, I want you to zoom through your qualification, stress-free.

Or, let's say your team has 10 bookings - but you personally only have 1. That falls short of your "Success formula" - and despite the fact that your team will achieve the sales goal - if you don't add more bookings to meet your personal sales, you probably won't meet the requirements (or in the future, get paid at title).

Watching these simple numbers constantly (I recommend weekly - but more about that later) is the way you transition to being a "business person" and it empowers you with information to make good decisions about managing your time and resources effectively.

Part Four: Team Sponsoring

Depending on your plan, and whether this is your first promotion or next promotion - you may not be *required* to have team members who sponsor new consultants to meet your promotion requirements.

(In my former company - two of my team members had to sponsor at least one consultant prior to entering qualification.)

That being said - the faster you teach your team members to start sponsoring - the more committed they are to their businesses.

I like to say, "It makes them stick."

Even if a person is earning a $10 commission each month on her team production, there's something about getting that ten bucks that makes a person stick around.

Plus - it makes perfect sense when you teach them the "Success Formula."

In my example, that formula was: *Complete 4 parties per month, sponsor 2 consultants per month, and teach everyone you sponsor to do the same thing.*

(See how this all ties together?!)

Later I'll be discussing a method for teaching team members to sponsor, AND holding them accountable for training their new team members.

But in the meantime - as you're gathering your data and making your strategic plan - find out how many prospects each of your team members is currently working with (if any).

Keep in mind consultants who aren't consistent with their bookings rarely focus or think about sponsoring. If they do sponsor a consultant, it often happens by accident.

That's because there's a little voice in their head that says, "This person is one of my best hostesses - and if I sponsor her, I will lose the parties she hosts a couple times a year."

The best way to help transition a consultant into a sponsoring mindset is to teach her how to fill her calendar with bookings consistently. More about this later.

Part Five: Promoting Leaders

If you need to promote leaders within your organization to earn your next promotion - this book (and frankly my "8 Weeks to Your Promotion Course" - 8WeekstoYourPromotion.com/course) are the perfect tools. Simply go back to the beginning of this book - and walk your future leaders through it - step-by-step.

I'm not going to spend a lot of time on this here - but once again, developing and promoting leaders is a process. Just like you have to plant seeds at parties to explain the benefits of being a hostess, you need to plant seeds continuously to develop leaders.

It's all about building their confidence, helping them learn the skills, inspiring them to think bigger, and showing them how easy it is to earn a promotion and maintain it.

Your Strategic Plan - a Quick Review

We've covered a lot - so let me do a quick summary of developing your strategic plan for earning a promotion - using a BALANCED approach:

1) You've reviewed and charted all of your qualification requirements, post-promotion requirements (to be paid at title every single month), and additional incentives (such as bonuses).

2) You've determined your "Success Formula" and, using your average party sales, calculated the number of bookings you need to personally complete each month to hit those sales.

3) You've also calculated the number of prospective team members you need to connect with each week, or each month, in order to personally sponsor a specific number of consultants (per your "Success Formula") into your business each month.

4) You have built a big prospective consultant list based on past hostesses, future hostesses, and past customers.

5) You calculated the total number of parties you and your team need to complete each month in order achieve your team sales requirements.

6) You made a chart of all the qualification/promotion requirements (across the top) - and listed each team member down the left side (starting with your personally sponsored consultants first, then the rest of your team), and checked off each requirement they meet, plus the number of parties each has booked for the upcoming two months; and the number of prospects each team member is currently working with.

7) You've totaled up your columns, and by comparing these numbers to your requirements, you have a clear picture of where to focus your efforts to be well-prepared for qualification.

Congratulations! You now have created a strategic plan.

Wherever the holes are - make a list of what you need to do to get those holes plugged!

Whether it's more bookings - personally or for your team - or more consultants - or higher sales per party - whatever your chart reveals to you - take action now.

These things don't have to take months. You can literally help consultants learn to book more parties, or you can learn how to approach prospects and sign new team members, in just a couple evenings if you're focused.

So get moving now. You have a promotion to earn!

How exciting are your dreams?
Most people don't aim too high
and miss, they aim too low and
hit.
- Bob Moawad

The Skills that you Need

In order to successfully achieve a promotion, there really are only three "essential skills" that you absolutely need.

Remember - everything - and I mean everything - in this business is a skill. Just like riding a bike - you might be a bit "wobbly" at first - or you might have "training wheels" for a period of time.

But once you get it - you get it.

The skills:

1) Learn how to book parties.

There is no shortage of hostesses. You might "think" there aren't a lot of potential hostesses - but in reality - they are everywhere when you learn this skill.

2) Learn how to coach your hostesses well.

In my world, hostess coaching is the beginning of the sponsoring process. Your hostess is your "business partner for the evening" and needs training. Teaching her how to be a great hostess is how you will have outrageous sales, lots of future bookings, and several business prospects. It's a very good investment of your time.

3) Learn how to sponsor new consultants well.

Obviously sharing the business with others is the way to build your organization. But to me, being a great sponsor starts when the new consultant signs. Learning to be a great trainer, coach and mentor is what really makes your business grow - and leaves you feeling great about what you do at the end of the day.

Are there other skills that can be helpful?

Absolutely. I know one of the reasons I was outrageously successful in my company is that I was always a student. I'm always reading books, taking courses, and anxious to learn something new or insightful.

Learn techniques for increasing sales at every party. Learn how to find business leads through social media. Use technology when it makes sense and supports business growth.

I also took what I learned and implemented it. Implementation is what separates those who achieve outrageous results from those who achieve mediocre results.

Most home part companies offer great training for their leaders. So focus first on achieving the promotion - then give yourself permission to learn to be a great leader.

Use the services of a good business coach. Someone who has been where you want to go.

I hired business coaches a couple different times, and it always helped me get past a growth plateau. Even now, I have a business coach (to the tune of about $1000 per month) who is helping me take my business to the next level.

You have permission to not be perfect. You have permission to learn.

Don't think you need to know everything to proceed. Just master the three skills: bookings, hostess coaching, and sponsoring quickly - and teach those skills to your team.

(When I talked about the behaviors that compensation plans are designed to encourage - these skills directly equate. Personal Sales (bookings and hostess coaching), Personal Sponsorships (sponsoring), Team Sales (teach them bookings skills and effective hostess coaching), Team Sponsoring (teach your team how to be great sponsors). Simple.

You've can do this! I know it!

Aim so high you'll never be bored.

- Linda Gibbons

What Do Your Team Members WANT? What Coaching and Training Do Your Team Members NEED?

When I first started working with one of my private coaching students, she was really "pushing" a couple of her consultants to earn their first promotion (and in turn, she would earn a promotion at the same time).

Remember - you have to stay focused on what *they* want - not what *you* want.

This all starts by having "real" conversations. Not through Facebook, not through text messages, not through emails.

It means picking up the phone and connecting.

You have to practice being a great listener. If not, your consultants will tell you what they think *you* want to hear - versus what they really really want.

Here's some ideas for questions that can help you get the conversation started.

Question Number One:

"If you think back to when you started your business - WHY did you start?"

Question Number Two:

"Is that still your goal - or do you have a new reason for being part of our company?"

Question Number Three:

"How can I help?"

Learn to diagnose where their businesses are stuck.

My favorite way is to figure this out - and help a consultant leap forward - is to attend one of their shows. You will learn amazing things about the coaching and training a team member needs when you attend and observe.

Another way to diagnose is to ask lots of questions. "Walk me through - from beginning to end - what happens at your shows..."

"What do you say to your hostess?" "How do you greet the guests?" How many samples do you take?" And so on...

I want to take a minute to talk about your "investment" in your new consultants.

I have hundreds - OK - thousands of students. One recent trend that frankly, surprised me, is how little time many consultants invest in helping a new consultant launch her business.

I know - most companies have great training in their back offices. (In fact, I believe that has compounded this issue. Sponsors are too often simply directing their new team members to "check out the training in the back office" instead of doing a lot of "hands-on" training.)

One of the big causes: "Short Term" versus "Long Term" thinking.

I often hear consultants complain that they can't commit an evening of their time to helping a new team member because they won't be the one bringing home the profits that night. (Some have even shared that they "make a deal" with the new team member - they keep the sales/profits - and she gets the bookings.)

That is "short term" thinking, versus "long term" thinking.

It's "short term money" thinking versus "lots of commissions over time" thinking.

What's most important when a new consultant starts her business?

She needs to feel confident in her decision. She needs to put bookings on her calendar - fast - to prove to herself (and her family and friends) that she can succeed.

The faster she starts making some party commissions herself - the more excited and more confident she'll be about her future in your company - *and as one of your team members.*

That's why I coach my students to do really strong launch parties with their team members - even before their kits arrive. Get them going fast.

You are NOT in the business of earning kits for people. But you ARE in the business of coaching, training and mentoring everyone you sponsor.

The time you invest in your new team members during this "development" stage will provide a huge return on that investment - for many years to come.

You know me - I'm going to give you some numbers.

Let's say that you help a new consultant do a launch party (5 hours of your time with coaching), attend a second party a month later (to help her increase sales, get more bookings, and spot prospects - 3 hours), and help her connect with a couple prospects (3 hours).

You have now invested 11 hours into this consultant, spread over a couple months.

(And by the way - she is now excited about sponsoring more team members - and you have set an example for her to do excellent coaching and training as well!)

Let's say in year one - this consultant averages $1000 in sales per month - and you're earning 5% commissions.

Over that year you will earn ($1000/month x 12 months x 5%) $600 in commissions from her production.

How does that $600 in commissions compare to the profits you might have earned at that initial party? Your commissions would possibly be $150-$200 - right?

Let's extend this out 5 years. And let's say you're now at the highest level in your company - earning 9% (in my example).

Now - you're earning $1080 per year from her production.

Yes - lots of assumptions - but here's the point.

Think bigger. Think long term return-on-your-time-investment versus short term cash-in-my-pocket-tonight.

Think about the potential income you can earn when your new team member has an "over the top" experience in her first couple months. Moves up the learning curve quickly, and starts building a team in your organization.

As you go through your list of team members - think back to their experience when they started their business.

I like to use my "Lather-Rinse-Repeat" formula and use that to find the holes in their business - starting from step one.

Would it help to do a "relaunch?"

If they never really got many bookings to start their business - help them "restart."

Are they doing well, but need some assistance booking more parties at their parties? Teach them the booking skills that you have now mastered yourself.

Are they doing lots of shows - but their sales at each show are "minimum parties?" Maybe they need to improve their hostess coaching skills. Or maybe they don't present the products well?

The point is - the way you build a strong team is to figure it out. Be like the "doctor" who has to ask lots of questions about your "symptoms" in order to figure out a "treatment plan."

I recently held a very successful 8-week class (it was called Party Plan Summer School), and prior to the start - I surveyed the students to learn what their biggest challenges were in their businesses.

Overwhelmingly - they were all having problems booking parties consistently.

You can fix that.

The second biggest problem: building productive teams.

Think about it for a minute. If you haven't mastered booking skills yourself - and then you sponsor team members and they, in turn, don't learn bookings skills - it has a huge trickledown effect.

Figure out what each team member needs, based on your conversations with her, then make a plan to give her the coaching and assistance she needs.

I used to separate my team members into "buckets" to give myself more clarity about the kind of training they needed:

Bucket #1 (and it will always be your biggest bucket) is for consultants who aren't consistent with their sales or bookings.

As I mentioned earlier - if a consultant isn't consistent with her own sales, she has a hard time sponsoring because she has concern that she will "lose" business.

This is also helpful training for consultants who need to "re-launch" their businesses (especially if you're a leader who needs to increase your team's production).

Training needed: Sales and Booking Skills

Some may benefit by "re-launching" their business; others need to learn how to get bookings at their parties; and others need to learn how to make calls to solidify dates for "call me next month" bookings.

When you focus on teaching the consultants in Bucket #1 bookings skills, it can have a big impact on your team sales.

Bucket #2: Consultants who are fairly consistent with their bookings (with sales per month achieving the minimum required to be paid at title) - but haven't sponsored team members - or at least more than one or two team members - yet.

These people need sponsoring training. Once they learn how easy sponsoring is, and how there are two or three (or more) hot prospects at every single party - they will start building like crazy!

When they learn this - they move to Bucket #3...

Bucket #3: Your future leaders.

They know how to sell; they know how to book; they know how to sponsor (and in that process learned how to coach and mentor their new team members well) - the next step is to earn a promotion.

Now you can use this book (or recommend they invest in my full "8 Weeks to Your Promotion" course).

If we did all the things we are capable of, we would literally astound ourselves.

Thomas Edison

How You Need to Distribute Your Time - Before, During and After Qualification.

Remember - it's all about balance.

(For those who are students in my "8 Weeks to Your Momentum" course, there's a great time management worksheet to download. It really keeps you focused on balance.)

First - how many hours do you have per week to commit to your business?

Ten - Fifteen - or more?

I don't "expect" you to commit more hours than you realistically have available. In fact, I'm all about figuring out ways to get bigger results in less and less time.

The goal is to help you *distribute* and *manage* the hours that you have so you're covering all the important business building aspects of your business.

Be realistic.

How many hours can you commit to your business each week?

_____

Divide those hours by the four important business-producing activities:

Personal Sales _____ hours
(Be sure to include time for hostess coaching, the party itself, and entering the order.)

Personal Sponsoring _____ hours

(This includes meeting with 1-or-2 prospects each week, time for coaching new consultants, and helping with launch parties.)

Team Sales _____ hours

(Depending on how long your team has been in their businesses, this might be helping with a re-launch party, providing booking training, or holding a team teleseminar or live meeting to increase their skills.)

Team Sponsoring _____ hours

(This could be helping a team member connect with a couple prospects, putting on an opportunity night, etc.)

If I had just 15 hours per week to work my business (think about it - that could be 4 hours two nights per week, and 7 hours on the weekend - OR - 4 hours Monday thru Thursday, leaving your weekends free, and so on), here's how I'd break it up:

Personal Sales: 5 hours

Personal Sponsoring: 5 hours (2 hours to connect with prospects *at appointments I booked right at my parties* - I don't want to play phone or message tag - and 3 hours to assist a new consultant with a launch party or coaching!)

Team Sales: 3 hours (preferably to attend/observe a party, or provide hands-on training)

Team Sponsoring: 2 hours

Get out your calendar and schedule time for each of these activities, every week during your qualification and promotion period (and beyond!).

Whatever amount of time you have for your business - make sure you use it well, and keep it balanced.

We are what we believe we are.

- Benjamin N. Cardozo

Are You Ready?

If you've "played along" through this section - you should have everything in place to evaluate where your business is at, what you need to do (both for your personal business and your team) to prepare for your qualification, and a clear understanding about whether you're ready to promote now. Or, if perhaps you need another month of development.

I believe you can achieve ANYTHING - if you're focused and take the right kind of action.

I'm not in any way suggesting that you should slow down your business.

But in my years of coaching consultants into, through, and post leadership promotions - I probably recommended that they give it "one more month" more often than I pushed.

Some took my advice. Others didn't.

Those who took that extra month sailed through their qualifications, like I did.

The others squeaked it out.

Another observation: those who sailed through their qualification went on to build $650,000 (our company's Circle of Excellence level) or even Million Dollar units.

Those who barely squeaked it out often stayed in the "make my numbers this month, not make them the next two," cycle.

Making a recommendation for a consultant to give herself one more month of development is tough. I equate it to the agony a few of my friends faced when they held their child back to repeat Kindergarten.

Years later, they all said it was the best decision they could have made for their child - but at the time - it was painful and difficult.

Unfortunately, your sponsor isn't always the best person to help you make this evaluation (sorry sponsors - you probably don't like hearing this).

Often, they get very excited that they'll be promoting a new leader - because when that happens, they'll earn a promotion, too.

I see it all the time.

They mean well, they're excited for you, they've probably put a good chunk of time into helping you develop your business.

But sponsors don't always look realistically at the numbers.

(That's why I dragged you through them in this section! I want you to make logical versus emotional decisions about this.)

A couple months ago, I got a text message from the sponsor of one of my private coaching students.

It was two days before the end of the month, and about three days before that - my student had sponsored another consultant to reach the required team size.

So the sponsor, salivating to earn her next promotion before her company's National Conference, coached my student to do a "hail Mary." She coached her to try to rally her team (using one of those "help me earn my promotion" pleas - something that does more long-term damage than good). (By the way - more about how to engage your team in the next section.)

The text I received from my student's sponsor said, "Your student is trying to promote this month - all cheers appreciated."

They weren't ready. My student and I had been focused on getting her personal business ramped up, and helping her brand new team members launch their businesses successfully. They needed another month.

They didn't make it.

But the next two months (her company has a two month qualification period), because her business was solid, she had helped her new team members launch their businesses successfully, and she knew exactly how many parties her team members had scheduled (more than enough to meet the requirements) - they successfully completed their promotion.

Review this section again…and then again.

Then decide if you're ready to go - this month - or next month.

Now…time to implement your plan and earn your promotion.

Courage is not the absence of fear, but rather the judgment that something else is more important than fear.

- Ambrose Redmoon

Part III: Implementing the Plan!

What You Focus on Is What You Get

I learned this lesson several years ago. What I focused on repeatedly with my consultants was exactly what I got.

Let me ask you a question. Let's say you love Mini Cooper cars as much as I do, and you start thinking about purchasing one. A blue one with a black roof to be exact.

Suddenly - everywhere you go - you start to see blue Mini Coopers with black roofs.

You didn't notice that many of them on the road before, but now it seems as though they are everywhere you go.

That's because you are focused on and thinking about Mini Coopers.

Here's just an example of what I mean by "focus."

You've mapped out your plan for earning a promotion, and based on the number of bookings you know the team needs to complete, it appears you're a bit short.

Now in your weekly calls to your team members - you ask, "Do you mind sharing with me - how many bookings do you have on your calendar in the next 6-to-8 weeks?"

If they have the number of bookings on their calendar that matches their goals - congratulate them and celebrate.

If not - you need to do some additional training.

After you get the booking numbers from the entire team - you post a note on your group Facebook page congratulating and listing each consultant who has at least 3 parties booked for the next month.

A team member posts a comment that she booked another party. You make a big deal about it.

Then, at the beginning of the next week, you make another round of calls and ask each consultant, "So how are the bookings coming along? How many shows do you have booked in the next 6-to-8 weeks?"

Do that for a few weeks in a row - and you will see your bookings increase.

You're focused on it, so that's what your consultants create.

When I made a decision to achieve my company's National Manager level, I needed to promote out seven managers. I talked about promoting to management constantly. I reviewed the requirements regularly. At every meeting, I asked team leaders to share their goal, and if they planned to go into qualification for management, the months they were targeting.

I focused on it, I matched the training and recognition with that goal, and gave lots of attention to those moving towards management.

It took a few months to get things rolling - and I continued my focus. Once the first manager went into qualification, within the next 12 month time-frame, I promoted six managers directly, and one indirectly.

Laser focus gets results. (And in the next couple days, I know you're going to see a lot of Mini Coopers, too.)

Nothing splendid has ever been achieved except by those who dared to believe that something inside them was superior to circumstances.

- Bruce Barton

Engaging Your Team

Yes - you are the person earning the promotion - but to do that - you need the support and participation of your team.

That means you need to communicate your goal; explain the requirements and the time-frame; ask for their full participation; and make sure each team member - whether she is making minimum orders or completing several shows per month - understands that she is important and appreciated.

What I have found to be most effective is to put together a team meeting, preferably prior to the start of your qualification month or months.

I recommend waiting for the meeting to explain that you're heading into qualification. That way it's a big surprise announcement.

Keep in mind - you've been a great coach, trainer and mentor. Your team members will be excited for you and they will want to help you succeed. Plus, it will inspire them to follow right behind you, if you keep the momentum building. (More about that later.)

If you have team members in other states - be prepared to bring them into the meeting via Skype or a Google Hangout. It's important is to get your entire team (if possible) together at the same time as you go through this information and ask for their participation.

I recommend that you invite each team member to your special team gathering through several forms of communication.

Here's some examples for your invitation:

a) Facebook group page

Hi Everyone! I have some really exciting news to share with all of you - so I'm hosting a special team meeting on (day, date) at my home (address). I am so grateful to have the opportunity to work with incredible women - like all of you! Can't wait to share the news. Please be sure to bring your calendars, and comment below to confirm you can attend.

b) Email

Hi Everyone! I have some really exciting news to share with all of you - so I'm hosting a special team meeting on (day, date) at my home (address). If you haven't already replied in the Facebook group - please reply to this email to let me know you can attend.

I am so grateful to have the opportunity to work with a team of incredible women - like you! Can't wait to share the news. Please be sure to bring your calendars.

c) Personal Phone Call

Just want to make sure you saw my Facebook post and email about the team meeting I've scheduled for (day, date). I've got some exciting news to share with everyone - can you attend?

To prepare for the meeting:

1)   Create a chart or handout (or both) to share with each team member that explains the requirements.

At the top of the chart list all qualification requirements.

As explained in the previous section, list what the sales requirement is equivalent to in total number of bookings that you and your team need to complete.

Next make a simple graph.

List the requirements across the top:

In my example that would be:

Team Member, Personally Sponsored, Qualified, Month 1 Bookings, Month 1 Bookings Goal; Month 2 Bookings, Month 2 Bookings Goal, Prospects.

Down the left side - start with your name. Enter the number of bookings you have in month 1, enter your month 1 bookings goal (even if it is the same or less than what you have booked), month 2 bookings, your moth 2 bookings goal (again, even if it is the same or less than what you already have booked), and the number of prospects you currently have on your prospect list that you are actively working with.

Next, list the team members' names you personally sponsored in order, starting with the consultant you sponsored first.

Finally, list the team members' names who have been sponsored into your team by others.

I like to cover up the chart with a piece of fabric, write the chart a couple pages in so I can flip to that page, to do a "big reveal" during the meeting.

Next - prepare some inexpensive, adorably wrapped, recognition gifts that include a personal note for every single consultant. (If you have consultants who are long distance, and can't attend the meeting, send these in advance with a note to wait for the meeting to open them.)

You want this recognition to be very specific (remember - what you focus on is what you will get!). Whether they just achieved their qualification, completed 2 parties in the previous month, had the highest sales on your team, sponsored their first team member, or simply placed an order to stay active (yes, you read that correctly - every team member needs to be recognized for whatever she is doing).

You want everyone to feel special and receive recognition.

At the meeting:

I know you're terrific at throwing a fun party. Your team members arrive, you serve some light refreshments.

I like to go around the room and ask each team member to introduce herself, and share why she started in the business, how her business is progressing, and any areas where she might need some additional help.

Next - give recognition gifts to every single team member. Make her feel special and appreciated - whether she is barely active or your top producer.

Start the recognition from "lowest to highest" meaning start with the barely active person - and end with the highest producer.

Then you share your big announcement.

For example:

"I'm excited to announce that, based on how well we are all doing with our businesses - I've set a goal for next month to be the start of my qualification for a promotion. Even though I'm the person who will earn the new title - qualification is a team effort. Based on your goals that you just shared, I know that many of you will be earning a promotion yourself in upcoming months - and I'm looking forward to helping you in any way that I can.

Let me start by reviewing the requirements - and getting more details about your bookings and prospects."

Make it clear how many bookings you need as a team, and the number of prospects you need to connect with and sponsor, as a team, to achieve the promotion.

Go through the chart, team member by team member.

First - share what you have happening in your business. (There's nothing more powerful than you showing what you've got on your calendar - and that you're "walking the talk.")

Next, go through each team member from top to bottom.

In my example:

Starting with the first team member.

If she's "qualified" - check that box. (Congratulate her!)

Ask how many bookings she has coming up in month 1 - enter the number. (Congratulate her again!)

Ask what her booking goal is for month 1 - and enter that number.

If her booking goal is bigger than what she has booked - explain that you'll be discussing more about this later, including ideas for everyone to increase their bookings.

Ask how many bookings she has coming up in Month 2 - and enter that number. (Yippee, etc.)

Ask what her booking goal is for Month 2 - and enter that number.

Finally - ask how many business prospects she is currently working with - and where each one is at in the decision process.

This is critically important: you must stay focused on appreciating what each person is doing. No one can leave this meeting feeling inadequate or unappreciated.

If they say their goal is one booking each month - and that's what they have booked - be grateful and thank them for being a great team member.

After you go through each team member's information - add up the columns.

Then compare the totals to the requirements to show the team where you're at. Let the numbers do the talking!

If you have more than enough bookings and prospects - fantastic.

If you are falling short - ask them to help!

In my example:

Previously I showed that with $500 average shows, 8 parties need to be booked each month to make the requirements.

If, between the future leader's booked parties and the team's booked parties there are 12 bookings on the calendar in month 1; 8 on the calendar for month 2; you are well prepared for entering qualification.

On the other hand, if your total team parties are at 6 - you've got some work to do to get the team prepared for your qualification and promotion period.

Now that you've reviewed the chart - have a brainstorming/training session about how each person can increase her bookings. Talk about each person's prospects and determine what each prospect needs to make a decision. That might be booking a party to "observe as if she were a consultant," or it might be you reaching out with a personal call.

Get ideas and engagement from the entire team.

Next - ask about every prospect that was mentioned on the chart. Find out how you can help turn those prospects into consultants.

By this time your team should be excited and engaged. They want to be part of a winning team. They want to help you achieve your promotion, and many will want to follow right behind you.

Finally explain how you will be communicating with them regularly throughout the qualification period (and beyond).

This is important.

Explain that you would like to schedule a regular time to connect with each team member **by phone** at the beginning of each week.

This call only needs to be five minutes each. (In fact, set a timer!)

Schedule that regular weekly phone appointment with each team member at this meeting.

These calls are critically important. You will learn so much more about what is going on with your team members when you have conversations, can ask lots of questions, can build her confidence, and help her get over some speed bumps.

Obviously you'll also post updates on your Facebook private group page, and through weekly emails.

End the meeting with a celebration toast! Thank everyone for attending.

On to the next step for implementing your plan.

The difference between what we do, and what we are capable of doing, would solve most of the world's problems.

- Mahatma Gandhi

Your Weekly Meeting with Your Boss (that's YOU!)

Based on your team meeting, and your personal calls and connections with each member of your team - you now have a clear understanding of what each team member wants from her business, where she is getting stuck, and the additional training and coaching she needs to take her business to the next level.

Every week, at the beginning of the week - from this day forward - leading up to, during your qualification period, and every week after that (in other words - for the rest of your business life) - you need to have a short 15-to-20 minute meeting with your boss. In other words - a meeting with yourself.

Knowing what is happening with your business - and with your team members' businesses is crucial for managing effectively.

(For those who are registered in the full "8 Weeks to Your Promotion" course - there's a great form to use for this weekly business evaluation time.)

I recommend that you schedule your "communication and connection" time with your consultants just prior to your "meeting with your boss" (i.e. your business planning meeting). That way you'll have the most current information about what is happening with each team member.

In addition, pull any helpful information from your back office. If you can access information about your team's booked party dates, past sales-per-party totals, business prospects - any information that is helpful - look that up prior to your weekly business planning time.

Just like you did prior to your team meeting, make the same type of chart so you have a very clear visual of where you're at, and what you need.

Start by reviewing your personal business. How many bookings on your calendar in the next 6-to-8 weeks? How many prospects are you working with? What does each prospect need to make a decision?

Next, list the same information about each team member. How many bookings does each one have coming up in the next 6-to-8 weeks; what are their sales-to-date for the month; and how many prospects are they working with.

Now that you've collected all of this information, evaluate your numbers, and create your action plan for the week - being realistic about the number of hours you can commit to your business.

Start with your own personal business - always.

If you don't have enough bookings, as determined in your "Success Formula" - that's your first priority on your action list for the week. Do whatever you need to do to add those bookings.

Your Second Priority - personally meeting with two prospects per week.

Third Priority - helping your personally sponsored team members launch their businesses.

Fourth Priority - helping at least one consultant take her business to the next level. That might be helping with a re-launch party; attending one of her parties; or helping her meet with a prospect. Figure it out and work it into your schedule.

Take the number of hours you can commit to your business - and divide them among these activities.

That's how you grow your business with a balanced approach, and that's how you build the momentum to soar through qualification, and keep right on going.

He who would learn to fly one day

must first learn to stand and walk

and run and climb and dance;

one cannot fly into flying.

- Friedrich Nietzsche

Tracking Your Progress and Communicating with Your Team

Now that you've had your "weekly meeting with your boss" - where are you at?

On track? Ahead of schedule? Or, will you barely squeeze it out?

Based on the data you collected - you will know where you're at, and you can be proactive.

First, you need to communicate (as promised) your progress to your team.

As promised, post an update on your Private Facebook Group; send out an email.

Recognize each team member who took action during the past week - whether it was a huge party, adding more bookings, sponsoring a new team member, or simply placing an order. Anyone who did anything needs to get a pat on the back!

Next, tell them where you're at in comparison to what you need. Be honest, and ask for what you need.

You've already got a plan in place to provide more training and assistance to one or two team members.

Figure out what will be most productive to produce the results you need.

For example, if you have a consultant who has set a goal to complete at least 4 bookings per month - and she only has two on her calendar - coaching and helping her improve her bookings skills now can result in two more bookings for your team each month.

Maybe she needs your help learning how to call prospective hostesses, or maybe she needs to learn how to ask for bookings at her parties. Through your weekly connection calls, you'll figure out what she needs.

Maybe you have a consultant whose goal is to start sponsoring. Investing a couple hours to help her meet with a couple prospects can break her loose and turn her into a sponsoring machine.

Use the data about what your consultants are doing, combined with what they have shared about their goals, to make strategic decisions about how to divide up your time.

Now reach out to the team member or members you're focusing on this week.

"Hi (team member), have you got a minute?

First - I want to congratulate you. I was looking at the back office - and I see that you had a $600 party last week. Well done!

I know you said your goal is to build a team and earn a promotion yourself - and based on your sales - you are on your way.

Are you ready to start working on your sponsoring skills?"

Now you ask specific questions to determine where she's getting stuck. Just like a doctor, you need to ask lots of questions about the "symptoms" in order to make a diagnosis about what her business needs.

"Tell me more about what happens at your parties. What kind of bids are you putting out? What are you saying at your closing table?

Are you following-up the day after your parties? What is happening when you sit down with a prospect?"

Then offer your help. Be prepared to do whatever will have an immediate impact on her results.

What's most important for you to understand is that you are powerful. Powerful beyond belief.

You can have a major impact on each of your team members' lives by helping them increase their business.

You do that by knowing what's going on and having real conversations.

That's also how you shift from "hobbyist" to "business woman."

The first step towards getting somewhere is to decide that you are not going to stay where you are.

- J. Pierpont Morgan

An Example of The Impact You Can Have on Your Business and Team Results - especially with a Strategic Approach:

I'm going to walk you through an example - not to overwhelm you with numbers, but to show you how easily you can have a huge impact on your business results.

The Example:

Part One: Increase Bookings per Consultant

Everything in the home party business starts with solid booking skills. Everything.

Let's say you have a team of 5 Consultants, averaging 2 parties per month, and sales of $300 per party.

5 x 2 x $300 = **$3000 in team sales**.

You decide to focus on increasing bookings, and you help each team member improve her booking skills - and the result is it increases their bookings to an average of 3 per month.

3 Consultants, completing 3 parties per month, with sales of $300 per party is:

5 x 3 x $300 = **$4500 in team sales**.

You've now increased your monthly team sales by 50%, from $3000 to $4500.

Part Two: Increase Sales per Party

Based on your personal results, and the data you've been monitoring for your team, you determine that working to increase each team member's sales at her parties will have a major impact on your team results (plus they'll be thrilled that they're making more money!)

You put on a special training, or work with each team member individually, to help her increase those sales.

What's an easy way to do that? Use the Lather-Rinse-Repeat formula to figure out what kind of training each team member needs.

Some might need to tune-up their hostess coaching, because they're getting low attendance at their parties. Others might need to do a better job with their presentation.

Your focus has paid off! Now each team member is averaging $600 in sales per party.

5 team members x 3 parties per month x $600 per party = **$9000 in monthly team sales.**

Congratulations! **You have just TRIPLED your team sales** - with the same number of team members.

Part Three: Bring on more team members.

Now that your team members are doing well with their bookings and sales, help each team member learn to sponsor.

You might need to help them sit down with a couple prospects, or they might need to learn how to ask people to look at the business at the closing table.

Think about it - if every team member simply sponsored one, your team will double in size. (Do you see why I love my "Success Formula?")

With your training and assistance, every team member sponsors a new consultant. Now you have 10 team members - and <u>their sponsor</u> teaches them how to book parties, and have terrific results at each party.

10 team members x 3 parties x $600 per party = **$18,000 in monthly team sales.**

Yes, this is simply an example. It is intended to show you the impact you can have on your business.

Collect good information each week and let the numbers guide your business decisions.

Never let your fears hold you back from pursuing your hopes.

- John F. Kennedy

Let's Review

This is where we're at for implementing your plan and earning your promotion:

a)   You evaluated what was happening with your personal business, and your team, and determined you could meet the requirements for achieving a promotion.

b)   You met with your team, shared your exciting news, got them engaged, learned more about their goals for their business, and found out how many shows they have booked, and prospects they are working with, compared to their goals.   You brainstormed ideas to increase bookings and sponsorships.   All consultants felt appreciated, and understand they are important to the team.

c)   You pull information each week, and have your weekly "meeting with your boss" to review what you've completed, what you and your team have booked, and what you still need to add (if necessary) to meet your promotion requirements.

d)   You create a weekly action plan, starting with your personal sales and sponsoring first; then assisting new consultants; and finally working to coach and mentor at least one of your team members, based on the data.

e)   You are clear that you are very powerful and can have a huge and rapid impact on your team's productivity when you choose the correct training for their needs.

Everything is on track.   You are confident that you will easily exceed all the promotion requirements, and life is good.

This is how you earn a promotion - stress free!

But what happens if you're not on track? What then? That's what I'm going to discuss in the next section.

Believe it!

High expectations are the key to everything.

- Sam Walton

Crunch Time

I hesitated to include this section, because based on what I've taught you, IF you follow my plan, you should cruise through your promotion period and keep right on going. It should be fun, it should be exciting, and it should be stress-free.

But not everyone takes this information to heart.

So for those who find themselves down to the wire, and falling short of their qualification requirements, here's some advice.

First - this is important - I want to review what you SHOULDN'T do. I have very strong opinions on these areas - and witnessed first-hand over the year how these kinds of activities negatively impact future leaders:

If you are short on your own personal sales:

You SHOULDN'T buy products beyond a reasonable amount of personal use.

If you have to "buy" your promotion - you will never feel good about it. You'll always have that little voice in your head saying "I didn't truly earn it" and it will always tarnish your future.

Remember - step one in earning a promotion is all about being solid with your own bookings and booking skills. Go back and master your booking skills first.

You SHOULDN'T ask any of your consultants to put a portion of their sales under your name.

That starts you down a slippery slope. You're in transition to leadership. A strong leader doesn't ask its team to help with her own sales.

You can easily generate additional sales by contacting customers, hosting parties yourself, or even hosting Facebook parties.

If you need more qualified team members:

You SHOULDN'T manufacture a "qualified consultant."

What I mean by that is you don't put your sales under her name or buy a bunch of products from her to get her there.

For long term success in this business - you coach, train and mentor people.

In my book, putting your sales under another consultant's name is not just cheating - it's downright unethical.

Again, there are many ways to help your team members boost their sales.

If you need more consultants:

You SHOULDN'T manufacture a consultant by paying for a kit for someone who has no intention of building a business to some level.

Prospects are everywhere. When Grandma who is in the nursing home shows up as a new consultant on your team - it's sending a message to your team that it's "tough" to find and sponsor new teammates. It's not.

Here's what you SHOULD do if you're down to the wire, and still need a lot of sales or new team members:

Call a team meeting by phone, or in-person.

Brainstorm ideas for adding more sales, or finding more prospects - or both - whatever it is that you need to accomplish.

You will come up with an amazing number of ideas for doing this "final days - big stretch."

As an example:

Sales - host your own party, do a "preview" party to book new hostesses and sell products (as quickly as tomorrow night), call all past customers for outside orders, host Facebook parties, book some fast catalog parties.

I'm sure you and your team will come up with many more ideas.

New team members - who is on your prospect list and your team's prospect lists? Connect, explain the benefits of starting their businesses now, and ask them to start! So often prospects are dangling out in the air. They need to be asked to start.

You also have prospects "hidden" in you and your team's customer lists. Start reaching out to share the business info, and bring them onto your team.

Again - I'm sure when you all brainstorm and share ideas - you'll be able to rapidly add new consultants.

Most of all - believe you can achieve it, and TAKE ACTION!

Life is short, so when you want something you really do have to go for it.

- Kate Winslet

Know Your Numbers, Track Your Progress, and Don't Leave Anything to Chance

In conclusion.

You've prepared well. Your team is excited and supporting you. You have the skills, the activity, and most of all - the power to speed past your qualification requirements successfully.

Based on what I've shared in the previous sections - everything is in place to achieve your promotion.

Watch the numbers and be proactive. You've got this!

I love those who yearn for the impossible.

- Johann Von Goethe

Part Four: Keep the Momentum Going

Congratulations! You've earned your promotion!

So what's next?

First - you keep doing what you did to prepare for and earn your promotion.

Keep doing your weekly "meetings with your boss," focusing on the number of bookings on your calendar, the prospects you're connecting with each week, the number of bookings each of your team members has on her calendar for the upcoming 6-to-8 weeks; and the prospects each team member is connecting with each week.

It's just another version of "Lather-Rinse-Repeat."

The biggest mistake new leaders make is they stop doing the activities they did to get into qualification and earn their promotion.

Don't make that mistake.

Instead, stay focused and act as though you're preparing for and entering qualification...again!

One way to do that is through a "promotion celebration party."

I will give you some ideas in the next section.

Things may come to those who wait, but only the things left by those who hustle.

- Abraham Lincoln

Your Promotion Celebration

This party - or team gathering - should serve several purposes.

First - and obviously - to show your gratitude to your team, congratulate them all, thank them for all their help and commitment, and ask "who's next?"

Second - to add more team members!

Ask each team member to invite a couple guests - especially their top hostesses during your promotion period. (I actually like to hold a contest. There will be a special gift for each consultant who brings at least one guest - and a bigger prize for the consultant who brings the most guests. These do not need to be expensive gifts. Just wrapped up in cute packaging!)

Teach your consultants how to invite their guests!

They need to be very clear about the purpose of the party.

Here's an example of how that conversation might go:

"Our team just earned a promotion - so we're having a special celebration party at our leader's home. I'd like to invite you to the party as my special guest, because your party really helped us with our goal. We're going to have a ton of fun. We'll also review the information about our business. Have you ever considered taking a closer look at our business info? This will be a great way for you to learn more. The party is (day, date, time). Can you make it? Why don't I pick you up and we can ride together."

This is one example of what I mean when I say "keep the momentum building."

Ideas for the Celebration Party:

Be prepared with inexpensive-adorably-packaged thank-you gifts, and be specific with your recognition.

Do introductions - and make every single person feel extremely special. (Even if it is a guest who purchased a $10 product during your qualification!)

Ask your consultants to share their story (why they started, why they stay, what they love about the business) during their introductions. (This is a great way to get the guests excited to learn more.)

Start your recognition with the guests. (Prior to the party, ask each consultant to give you specific information about each guest they've invited - so you can give recognition.)

"Guest A - my gosh - you had a $1200 party - that is fantastic. What did you do with all of your hostess rewards?" Then, plant a seed. "Hostesses like you make incredible consultants - so I'm excited that you'll learn more about our business a little later."

"Guest B - did you know that (Team member C) booked 3 parties from your party? Your friends obviously LOVE our products!" Then you can say, "That's the reason many of our consultants get started in our business. They realize that their friends are all booking parties because they love our products so much."

Note: my "language" is planting seeds - not twisting arms.

Next, move onto your team recognition.

"Team Member A - completed the most parties during our qualification." Then add, "I'm betting that you will be the next person in our group to earn a promotion!" (Yes, I'm already going to start planting seeds to build leaders.)

"Team Member B - had the highest sales at a party during qualification." Then add, "Who knows - you might even earn a promotion at the same time as Team member A."

"Team Member C - is most improved. Went from barely staying active to completing 3 parties during qualification." Then add, "Keep building your business at this pace, and start sponsoring your team - and you can be in qualification very quickly."

"Team Member D - sponsored 2 new consultants and coached them so well - they are already qualified." Then add, "Do you realize that you could be in qualification yourself in the next month or two?"

"Team Member E - signed up under Team member D just a few weeks ago and qualified during our promotion period. You are off to an incredible start. You have a fabulous sponsor - and you've done a great job launching your business. Keep right on going and be the first leader to promote under Team Member D!"

And so on.

Next - after the recognition and toast to the team - explain that it's an incredible time to get started in your company (any day of the year is an incredible time to get started, in my world).

Take 15 minutes to review the information about your business and invite the guests to join your team.

People want to be part of a successful team. Here you are celebrating a promotion, and telling each team member how much you believe in her, and how she can be next to earn her own promotion. That can be very exciting and attractive to prospects.

You want to keep your momentum going. Think about it. If every team member sponsors one new consultant - you have now doubled your team size.

When I work with my private coaching students - doubling the size of their team is one of our first priorities. It should be yours, too.

Your dreams are alive. They live through you. Take good care of them.

- Kobi Yamada

Shameless Self Promotion

You earned the promotion. You deserve the promotion.

Now it's time to let others know about your success.

Update your images on your Facebook pages, websites, or anywhere you have images that include your title.

Update your title on all social media sites.

Post a note about your promotion in Facebook groups and all social media sites where you actively participate.

Send an email blast to all of your customers and hostesses - sharing the story of your successful promotion and thanking them for helping by being great hostesses and customers.

Send a press release to your local community newspaper. (Make sure you include your contact information so they can interview you, if they choose!)

You're going places in the business. Don't keep that a secret.

Destiny is not a thing to be waited for, it is a thing to be achieved.

- William Jennings Bryan

Part Five: If I Check In with You - 3 Months from Now - Will You Be Able to Tell Me that You've Earned a Promotion?

I sure hope so.

But, if not - why not?

I've walked you through exactly what you need to do - step-by-step. I've explained, in great detail, the exact process I used to develop and promote the most leaders of anyone in my former company.

There is no reason to build this business S-L-O-W-L-Y.

I know you have the very best intentions...but the truth is...good intentions are not going to get you there.

Most consultants need someone to keep them from getting sucked off track. They need friendly accountability. They need a coach and mentor.

It doesn't matter where you're at in the business.

Maybe you're new in the business - and have no direct sales experience.

(Actually, that's a benefit - no "old baggage" to deal with.)

I KNOW if you follow my plan, you can earn a promotion quickly.

Let me tell you about one of my private coaching students, Tara Murray.

From the first day she joined Stella & Dot, Tara Murray set a goal to earn promotions, and move up her company's compensation structure quickly.

Tara has no previous experience in direct sales. She and her family (her husband, a pastor, and her young son) recently returned to the U.S. after living in London for a few years where Tara, who is also a lawyer, worked on human rights issues.

Tara was literally starting from scratch - and began the year (which was just her 3rd month in the business) with no bookings on her calendar, and a couple of team members (her sister and some friends).

To get Tara prepared for a promotion - we had to start with her personal business - especially with her bookings.

Tara had to learn how to make connections, get them excited about the products, and then book shows. She also had to learn how to get future bookings AT her shows.

As Tara learned these skills herself, she also worked closely with her team members to pass along what she was learning.

In April (now her sixth full month in her business) she sponsored 3 new team members - and her sponsor got excited. Rightly so. Great sponsors love it when their team members are doing well - plus Tara's promotion would also help her sponsor earn a promotion.

Tara's sponsor wanted her to push and earn a promotion in May. I felt Tara needed to give her team one more month of development (based on her numbers) - and that's what she chose to do.

Tara scheduled her team meeting (including several of her team members live in different states) to share her goal of promoting to Star Stylist in June.

"My team got excited. I think it was encouraging for them, because I hadn't been in the business all that long," Tara said.

In fact, she explained that the Star Stylist level is known as the "sweet spot" in Stella & Dot. It's a coveted level within the company.

"For my team to see that someone who had just joined the company a few months earlier was ready to earn a promotion - it showed them what they can do with their business, too," Tara said.

Tara and her team focused and took action - not without a few "speed bumps" along the way - and she earned her promotion.

Her takeaways:

1) Even though her sponsor wanted her to promote in May (and Tara loves her sponsor, said she's been a great coach and has the utmost respect for her) - after reviewing the numbers, Tara waited a month and focused on getting more bookings, helped her team learn to book more shows, and added even more stylists to her team. That positioned her team much better for promoting in June.

2) She stayed in regular contact with the Stylists on her team. That gave Tara great information about where to focus her energy and time, along with areas where they needed some additional training.

3) Be prepared to shift when necessary. Tara and her team started the month with more than enough bookings, but some of them were rescheduled. At the end, she and her team got very creative. Tara did several Facebook parties, and when she was asked to go to New York to help her Mom move, they put together a show at the last minute (and it was over $1000 in sales, she booked two more shows, and one of the guests went online and signed-up on Tara's team as a complete surprise).

Most of all: Focus and Believe that earning your promotion is possible.

With the help of her team, Tara successfully earned her promotion, and is now focused on helping her team members do the exact same thing. She's not just a star - she's a superstar!

Tara Murray - Star Stylist
email: primpolishedpizzazz@gmail.com
FB page: https://www.facebook.com/primpolishedpizzazz;
web: www.stelladot.com/primpolishedpizzazz

As you can see from Tara's story - even if you're new in the business, you can focus on the right activities, learn the skills you need to learn, and earn a promotion in your first year - like Tara did.

Maybe you have an extremely busy life...like my private coaching student Helene Leonard.

Helene Leonard is a school teacher, a busy Mom of two young children, the wife of a police officer (whose schedule changes constantly), and an Independent Director with ThirtyOne Gifts.

She is absolute proof that you can have a crazy busy life, but with a strategic approach - can still earn a promotion, and keep your business growing.

"I'm efficient in building my business," Helene said. "I only spend time on things that are going to help me build my business - plus it doesn't take as much time as you think. It really doesn't. I think a lot of people think 'leadership' means a ton of time - it's a little more time - but not a ton more."

Helene shared that earning a promotion has not been exactly what she expected.

"It actually blew me out of the water because it is so much cooler than I expected. it turned out to be way better.

I didn't realize the impact I can have on people's lives. I didn't realize the skills I already had that I've been able to use. It's been a major blessing," Helene said.

Helene shared with me the 3 biggest lessons or take-aways and it's great advice since she promoted recently.

1)   Don't overthink it.

2)   Keep it simple.

3)   Keep the momentum moving - don't get complacent.

That's exactly what she did! Helene doubled the size of her organization in her first two months as a Director.

Helene will already be promoting her first Director in her organization in the next month or two. She is building her business on purpose, strategically, and loves helping people.

Helene Leonard
Independent Thirty-one Director
Rockaway, NJ
www.mythirtyone.com/helene
hsleonard@yahoo.com

Maybe you are one of those consultants who has achieved a promotion - and lost it?

I know - that's really really frustrating and discouraging.

I'm sure you learned a lot from that experience, and I know that it can be frustrating - but it doesn't have to define your future in your business.

Meredith Yost, another one of my private coaching students, had earned...and lost...a promotion. But that hasn't stopped her. Here's her story:

Meredith Yost was in my sales unit in my former company, so it was a huge compliment when she became a private coaching student.

She had a very demanding full time job, so prior to retiring from that job earlier this year, she worked her WineShop at Home business very part-time, and in many respects, inconsistently.

Before she started in my private coaching program, Meredith qualified as a leader - then lost that status just four months later.

"I didn't have the training or the time. The team slacked off. Then it just fell apart," Meredith said.

When I work with a private coaching student, the first place we have to start is by getting their own personal business "tuned-up." We start with consistent bookings. Next - good sponsoring skills. Next - developing new team members effectively. And so on. It's very strategic.

Meredith was making great progress down this path - and I knew she would be prepared to earn her first promotion within a couple months.

So imagine my surprise when I got a text from her sponsor (a fabulous woman who was also in my downline in my former company) two days before the end of the month saying "Meredith is working to promote this month and they have a ways to go. All cheers appreciated."

Our coaching calls are once a week. Based on the numbers (and this is probably the most important statement in the entire book - "based on the numbers") Meredith's team wasn't ready - yet.

The second she sponsored her 3rd Consultant - the number of personally enrolled consultants needed, along with other requirements, to promote to Leader in her plan - her sponsor got excited about earning a promotion herself and challenged Meredith to rally her team (I like to call this a "Hail Mary.").

I've seen that kind of "rally" many dozens of times over the years - and it rarely works for the long-term. In fact, it often does more harm, than good.

The numbers weren't there.

As you now know (if not, please review the second section), knowing how many bookings you need each month (both personally and as a team) is step one. Meredith's team didn't have the bookings.

Sponsors' hearts are in the right place. They are excited to help team members. They are anxious to earn their next promotion. In this case, it was also motivated by wanting recognition for promotions at their upcoming conference.

But the numbers don't lie. They weren't ready. And, they didn't make it. Strike two.

But one short month later it was a different story.

(It doesn't take years - they simply needed another month of development time. Especially her new consultants.)

Both Meredith and her team had the bookings. One of her consultants sponsored a new team member - so the team was bigger.

They successfully completed both months of the promotion, and she's a new leader.

What's most important is Meredith is continuing to grow. She's remaining consistent in her business, and monitoring what is happening every single week.

Here's Meredith's advice for anyone who has achieved a promotion, but couldn't maintain it, or didn't make it in their first attempt:

"Don't give up! Get focused, sit down and look at why you didn't make it the first time. Have fun and spend time together with your team!"

Meredith is now consistent, she is training and coaching her team members well, and her organization will continue to grow and expand. Well done!

Meredith Yost
Independent Leader
WineShop at Home
email: wineshopper4u@comcast.net
http://www.wineshopathome.com/meredithyost

I want to help you create your plan, implement it efficiently and effectively, and with the help of your team, sail through qualification.

I want you to have fun. I want it to feel powerful and invigorating, and feel absolutely great.

Your promotion can be completed easily, and without stress.

Too often, consultants, like you, have the very best intentions…but it's too easy for them to be sucked off track.

That doesn't have to be your story.

I want to be your coach and mentor.

I am so fortunate to have amazing private coaching students (who, these days, pay me up to $2497 every 3 months) - but at this time, that program is full.

I'd be happy to put you on a waiting list, but I must confess, most of my students have locked into the program for an entire year - so that could be a long wait.

So the best way I can help you take your business to the next level, and earn the promotion you deserve, is through my new "8 Weeks to Your Promotion" online course.

In the course, you'll simply walk through, step-by-step, taking everything you've just learned in this book and implementing it quickly - because you'll have specific training modules, great tracking forms, handouts, and me as your personal coach and mentor through a special Private Facebook group.

(For more information on my "8 Weeks to Your Promotion Course," go to: <u>8weekstoyourpromotion.com/new-course</u>)

Maybe you've already earned a promotion.

If you have, congratulations!

Frankly, I think leaders actually need my new course, "8 Weeks to Your Promotion" the most.

The only way to get to the top of your compensation structure (and on track to building a six figure or higher income) is by promoting leaders.

Leaders promote leaders.

It's also a skill that you need to master - like I did.

Let me tell you about Susan Milliron.

Susan Milliron is, at the time of this writing (I say that because her business is growing fast - so her title will be changing frequently), a Sr. Leader with Ruby Ribbon.

I knew Susan from my former business. She was indirectly part of my downline, and attended many of my training events. Frankly, I was surprised when she asked about being in my private coaching program.

She has 19 years of direct sales experience, and she was successful in her former companies. But she hadn't built organizations that went to the very top of the compensation plan.

This time, things are different. Susan is learning the skills, and focusing on building leaders. She has a clear vision that she can build her business to the very top, and it will provide the kind of income she has always been dreaming about - and deserves!

When she started in my private coaching, we had to give her personal business a minor "tune-up," and then we went to work on how she was communicating with her team, how she was approaching her business growth, and now - how she's building leaders.

Her biggest lesson, when it comes to building leaders, has been learning to separate those who really want to earn a promotion, from those who talk big, but take little action.

"Lots of people say they 'want' to be a leader - but not everyone is willing to do the work to achieve the promotion," Susan said.

Referring to the leader she most recently promoted, Susan explained: "Heather gets it. She makes sure that her calendar is booked with 6-to-8 bookings in the upcoming six weeks. She communicates regularly with her team members. (And by the way, none of her team members have previous direct sales experience.) Plus - she is coachable, and communicates with me regularly."

Heather's success is a direct reflection of Susan's coaching and mentoring. Susan is now focused on building leaders. and her organization is very quickly approaching exponential growth. Susan is spectacular, and she will be among the top leaders in Ruby Ribbon for many years to come.

Susan Milliron
rubyribbon.com/SusanMilliron
saybyebyebra@gmail.com

I want you to be the leader of an organization that everyone wants to join - because they know you'll help them succeed!

I want to make sure you're not "pushing" your team members into qualification before they're ready - it's the second biggest mistake leaders make.

At the same time, I want to make sure you're not holding someone back because you know if they promote, you won't have a strong team left.

(Go to: 8weekstoyourpromotion.com/new-course/ for all the details)

It doesn't matter if you can commit just 12-to-15 hours per week, or can work your business full-time.

What matters is how you use the time that you can commit, doing the right activities.

Let me share Dondrea Bryant's (another private coaching student) story:

Dondrea Bryant is a Sr. Director with ThirtyOne Gifts. She's a stay-at-home Mom of two busy kids, and her husband works crazy hours with his job (so crazy that Dondrea rarely schedules anything for her business on week nights, and when she does, has several sitters on alert in case her husband can't get home on time).

She started her business to make some extra cash to "fund her Target addiction." But her business rapidly grew way beyond that initial goal.

"I had a mindset that it was going to be extremely difficult - I thought it was going to take a lot of time, energy and hours. It doesn't. As long as you manager your time effectively, you can be a leader without it taking a ton of time. That was very eye opening," Dondrea said.

Now Dondrea is at a new place in her journey. Just like consultants learn how to book parties and connect with prospects - promoting Directors and building leaders is also a learning stage of your business.

"I learned I had to allow my leaders to spread their own wings and take on their own team - just like I'm responsible for taking on my own team. I'm still there to help and support them - but they have to be the leader of their team," Dondrea said. *"Learning that was a huge relief. I really did feel that I was responsible for everybody. Realizing they have to be responsible for their own team was such a huge weight off of my shoulders. It was so much more manageable to concentrate on my 'several handfuls as opposed to the bucket full."*

Dondrea earned Thirty-One's leadership incentive trip for both she and her husband her first year as a Director.

She had a repeat performance in year two - and earned the leadership incentive trip for both of them, as a Sr. Director.

Dondrea's advice for leaders who are ready to start promoting leaders themselves: "Be real. Have real conversations with people about the business and tell it like it is - don't sugar coat anything. You will be amazed what can come out of it."

Her business is on fire - and I'm confident she will soon be among the Senior Executive Directors in her company.

Dondrea Bryant
Independent Sr. Director, Thirty-One
https://www.mythirtyone.com/dondrea
dondreabryant@gmail.com

In addition to the training modules, the tracking forms (that are extremely helpful), and the handouts, one of the big benefits of being part of my family of students in my "8 Weeks to Your Promotion" course is the Private Facebook group.

First - you get to "hangout" with consultants who are really going places in their businesses. They are all there to earn their first - or next - promotion.

Who better to share ideas with, post questions to, and share your success stories with, than with an entire group of consultants who are focused on earning promotions?

Plus - I go into the Facebook group 2-to-3 times per week and add my "2-cents."

(Go to: <u>8weekstoyourpromotion.com/new-course</u>/ to invest in this program - and to take your business to the next level - NOW.)

You deserve this. Time to dream big and take action. I'd love to be your coach and mentor.

Big Hugs,

Susie

About the Author

Susie Nelson built, and maintained, one of the top organizations in her home party sales company and became its second Independent National Sales Manager (a level that was only reached by six consultants in the history of the U.S. company).

From the day she made the decision and commitment to build her business and organization to the top level in her company, and to create a six-figure+ residual annual income, Susie focused her efforts, developed and implemented a strategic plan, and created systems to build her business quickly.

All of those efforts paid off. Here's just some of Susie Nelson's accomplishments:

- Under Susie's direction, her organization achieved her company's "Circle of Excellence" award every single year. To do that, a unit had to achieve at least $650,000 in sales. Eight of those years, her unit exceeded $1 Million in sales, and one year – they even exceeded $2 Million in sales.

- Susie promoted the most sales managers of anyone in the U.S. company – 16 to be exact. (To become a sales manager, you had to build and maintain a unit of at least 20 party plan consultants, and exceed $7000 wholesale production per month.) She also inspired 2 women to become sales managers indirectly (meaning, one of her off-spring managers promoted those managers within 12 months of becoming a sales manager herself).

- She became her home party sales company's 2nd National Sales Manager (only six managers achieved this level). This level was achieved when you promoted at least 10 sales managers from your unit.

- Susie was awarded the company's President's Award (based on production, growth, attitude, and votes from her peers) twice. This award was only given to four consultants per year – so to receive this recognition twice was an incredible honor.

- In 1996, Susie was also recognized for "Most Sales Manager Promotions" for promoting out 6 sales managers in a single year – a record that was never broken. She is extremely proud of this accomplishment – because she believes that home party and network marketing businesses are built by coaching, training and mentoring others. Many of her off-spring managers went on to build Million Dollar and $650,000 units themselves.

- Susie served on the company's "Manager Panel" four different calendar years – a group of top sales managers that met regularly with the President and V.P. of sales to provide ideas and give feedback about business development.

- Susie built and maintained a 6-figure income ($105,000 to $135,000) for 11 years straight! Not many consultants in the party plan industry achieve that level of financial success. She credits implementing a smart, well-planned business strategy, along with creating systems in her business for helping her develop a strong organization.

She has also worked on the corporate side of the business – for 3 different start-up companies, doing everything from developing comprehensive training programs, field development, and marketing.

Susie is the author of 3 books:

"I Did It, and You Can, Too: How to Build a Six Figure Direct Sales Business in Just 15 Hours Per Week." (Available on Kindle, or PDF)

"The Pros and Cons of Building More than One Direct Sales Business: What You Must Consider Before You Sign with a Second (or Third!) Company." (Available on Kindle, or PDF)

"8 Weeks to Your Promotion In Your Home Party Business: How to Rapidly Qualify for a Promotion, and Get Paid at Title Every Single Month."

Now Susie has a new goal: **To help at least 1000 home party consultants build a six-figure business, using her proven systems and strategies.**

Dreams take long term commitments. From the first to the last, we need focus, discipline, persistence, and the ability to keep sight of the vision of what we are slowly creating.
Dennis Wholey

To Contact Susie Nelson:

email: Susie@SusieNelson-Training.com

37284738R00096

Made in the USA
Charleston, SC
03 January 2015